The
Rookie
Manager

The Rookie Manager

A Guide to Surviving Your First Year in Management

JOSEPH T. STRAUB

AMACOM

American Management Association

New York • Atlanta • Boston • Chicago • Kansas City • San Francisco • Washington, D.C.

Brussels • Mexico City • Tokyo • Toronto

This publication is designed to provide accurate and authoritative information in regard to the subject matter covered. It is sold with the understanding that the publisher is not engaged in rendering legal, accounting, or other professional service. If legal advice or other expert assistance is required, the services of a competent professional person should be sought.

Library of Congress Cataloguing-in-Publication Data

Straub, Joseph T.
    The rookie manager : a guide to surviving your first year in management / Joseph T. Straub.
      p. cm.
    Includes bibliographical references and index.
    ISBN 0-8144-7060-2
    1. Supervision of employees. 2. Middle managers. 3. Executive ability. 4. Management I. Title.
    HF5549.12.S77 1999   *99-33979*
    658.4—dc21   *CIP*

Printing number
10 9 8 7 6 5 4 3 2

For my wife, Pat, and our daughter, Stacey,
with all my love.

Contents

Chapter 1

Put on Your Manager's Hat

Congratulations on your promotion! It's exciting, challenging, and perhaps a bit unsettling. Even though you've dreamed about and worked toward it for a long time, knowing that you've reached a higher rung on your personal success ladder naturally brings a touch of anxiety.

A New Point of View

It's a big step up to the management level, and you may feel a little uncomfortable at first. Keep in mind, though, that culture shock hits everybody the first time he or she is promoted into supervision, so you're not the Lone Ranger. People grow only by being challenged, and every manager who ever lived has felt like you do now, thought many of the same thoughts and shared many of the same concerns.

There's more good news, too. Someone believed you were qualified to handle this promotion. Someone had enough confidence in your judgment to grant you this opportunity to stretch your wings and reach beyond your former rank-and-file job. Somebody believed in you at least as much as you believe in yourself. So rest assured that you didn't get where you are today by accident. You were most likely rewarded for the self-motivation, performance, and determination you displayed as a major contributor to the success of your organization.

So while you're thinking about your newfound responsibilities and the changes you'll experience in the days and weeks to come,

1

remember to celebrate the likely fact that you *deserved* your promotion. You've earned this new opportunity! If that weren't true, you wouldn't have it.

The Roles of a Manager

Management authority Henry Mintzberg has identified ten potential roles that you'll be called on to play and placed them into three general categories. See Figure 1-1.

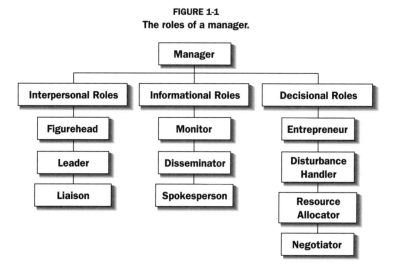

FIGURE 1-1
The roles of a manager.

Interpersonal Roles

Roles that relate to your relationships with others are considered interpersonal roles. They arise directly from your formal position and authority.

■ *Figurehead*. Managers are the heads of their own divisions, departments, or sections, and this means they must routinely perform certain ceremonial duties. For example, they may be required to conduct tours of their facilities, speak to service clubs and civic organizations, and attend employees' retirement dinners.

■ *Leader*. Managers are expected to create and maintain a positive and productive work environment for themselves and their employees. They play this role by attempting to improve employees' performance, reduce conflict, provide feedback on performance, and encourage their employees' growth and development. This leadership role will be explored further in Chapter 4.

■ *Liaison*. Managers interact with many other people besides their superiors and team members. These people include peer-level managers and employees in other departments, staff specialists, and external parties such as customers, suppliers, and representatives of government agencies.

Informational Roles

Managers often have more information than their employees, which is partly because of their network of contacts inside and outside the organization. Informational roles relate to using and disseminating information.

■ *Monitor*. Managers must constantly monitor the work environment to know what's going on. They collect information both by asking questions and by taking note of unsolicited information that comes to them through formal means (such as meetings, memos, and reports) and informal means (the grapevine, rumor, and other unofficial sources).

■ *Disseminator*. Managers act as disseminators when they relay information to their employees that the employees may not receive by other means.

■ *Spokesperson*. Managers are expected to speak for their work unit to people outside the work group. These people may include higher managers, peers in other departments, and various parties outside the organization.

Decisional Roles

Part of a manager's job is making choices. Managers may make decisions themselves (sometimes with input from others) or influence the decisions of others in the following roles.

■ *Entrepreneur*. Managers play an entrepreneur's role when they are exposed to new ideas and techniques that could improve their work group's productivity or efficiency. The entrepreneurial role requires managers to initiate activities that will encourage their employees to use these new ideas and techniques to maximum advantage.

■ *Disturbance handler.* When equipment breakdowns, strikes, scheduling problems, and other unpleasant surprises occur, managers are expected to develop effective solutions and keep their work groups moving forward.

■ *Resource allocator.* Managers typically are responsible for deciding how scarce resources such as money, materials, time, and equipment will be distributed among the members of their work group.

■ *Negotiator.* Managers often spend a good part of their time negotiating contracts with suppliers and bargaining with their peers in *Godfather* fashion for limited resources. This negotiator role demands that they have both the information and the authority to play it successfully.

Management Skills

Managers who hope to play the above roles effectively must also develop three types of skills: technical, human relations, and conceptual.

Technical Skills

Skills that are considered technical enable managers to use the processes, practices, techniques, and tools of the specific area that they supervise. For example, a manager who supervises accountants must know accounting. Although managers don't have to be hands-on technical experts (some fields, especially in high technology, change so fast that this becomes impossible), they must have enough technical savvy to direct employees, organize the work, communicate their work group's needs to others, and solve problems.

Human Relations Skills

Managers with sound human relations skills are able to interact and communicate with other people successfully. They understand, work compatibly with, and relate to both individuals and groups.

Conceptual Skills

Some skills enable a manager to view the organization as a whole and understand how its various parts relate to and depend on one another. Such conceptual skills deal with ideas, abstract relationships, and the ability to visualize how all parts of an organization might be reorganized to function more productively or at a lower cost. These skills enable a manager to see both the forest and the trees and to grasp the impact that his or her actions will have on other parts of the organization. See Figure 1-2.

FIGURE 1-2
Relative amounts of skill used at each level of the management hierarchy.

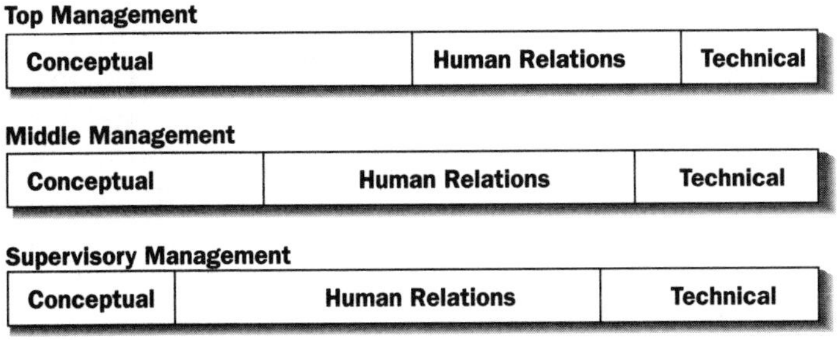

Top Management

Conceptual	Human Relations	Technical

Middle Management

Conceptual	Human Relations	Technical

Supervisory Management

Conceptual	Human Relations	Technical

The importance of each of these skills varies according to management level. For example, technical skills are critical for first-line managers, but they become less important as a manager is promoted up the ladder. Human relations skills are important at every level, but especially so for first-line managers because of the many different people they must deal with both above and below them. Although conceptual skills are least important for first-line managers, they become extremely important for those who advance to higher levels. Top managers are deeply involved with broad-based, long-range decisions that affect the entire organization. Indeed, managers who don't develop these conceptual skills will probably not advance very high. Their limited perspective will retard their success.

Changing Your Viewpoint

You'll be challenged not only to feel comfortable in your new role but also to alter your view toward your work and your organization. More specifically, new managers must train themselves to:

■ Define and solve problems and approach opportunities from management's side of the desk.

■ Broaden their perspective to see the "big picture" as it's relayed and projected from higher management.

■ Balance feelings of loyalty to their employees with loyalty to their supervisors, which is a responsibility that comes with the territory of management, no matter what level you're on.

Communicating Up the Ladder

Before you entered management, you may have worried mostly about understanding your boss's directives and carrying them out to the best of your ability. Now you must become a pipeline for communication that flows both up and down. Your employees will expect you to relay their ideas, concerns, and problems to managers above you; represent them clearly and fairly; and generally "be a good boss" (which each of your employees may define differently, but more on that later). You must also communicate information from your level that helps managers above you plan, organize, direct, and control the activities of all the departments within the organization.

But as a supervisor, you must also acknowledge, relay, and implement the goals and plans of managers above you through the people who work for you. This means you must reconcile demands and expectations that may conflict or operate at cross-purposes. This, too, is part and parcel of every manager's job.

Coping With Managing Former Peers

The odds are that several coworkers were also considered for your promotion, but you walked away with the prize. Don't be surprised if they express jealousy or resentment. The same qualities that earned you your job should serve you well here, however. Insulate yourself against petty complaints, backbiting, or gripes from colleagues who were passed over. Be objective, be fair, and be focused on making the most of your new career opportunity and confirming higher management's opinion that you were indeed the best candidate for the job.

In addition to deflecting former peers' resentment, you must resist their attempts to manipulate you, compromise your performance standards, or otherwise bend the rules "for old time's sake." You'll be challenged to be fair but firm, and do what's best for the entire organization and for the management team of which you're now a part. This doesn't mean you should become aloof or withdrawn or appear to let your promotion go to your head. It does mean, however, that you're no longer "one of the guys."

And if You're Not Managing Former Peers?

If you're supervising employees whom you haven't worked with before, go out and talk to them—more important, *listen* to them—about the nature of their jobs, the overall state of your department, and any special concerns they may have.

Listening doesn't cost; it pays. Managers who ask for advice or opinions demonstrate wisdom by admitting that they don't have all the answers. Moreover, your team members will be more willing to overlook your mistakes if you give them a fair audience and respect their opinions from the first day.

Consider meeting members of a new group on their own turf. They'll speak more candidly and comfortably than if they are "summoned" to your desk or cubicle. Sound out their feelings about work problems, their suggestions for improvements, and their opinions about such matters as work layout, equipment, training, and other issues that you may need to deal with once you've settled into your job.

You may want to review your employees' personnel files before you meet them to get a sense of their background, experience, previous assignments, and special skills. You'll also learn personal data that may help you establish rapport with them more easily.

Above all, reserve judgment on a new group of employees until after you've seen them from several sides and worked with them for several weeks.

Use Former Bosses as Guides

Invest some time evaluating and reflecting on traits that helped your previous bosses succeed and those that may have held them back. This may produce one of the best lists of do's and don'ts you'll ever find. Ask yourself questions such as:

■ How well did they communicate with others? What specific things did they do with regard to giving instructions, listening, asking and answering questions, disciplining, announcing bad news, following up, and the like that worked especially well (or not so well)?

■ How did they handle crises and react to bad news?

■ Which ones were exceptionally good at motivating their team members? What did they do that made this so?

■ Which former managers were especially savvy about managing their time? What principles and practices did they use to help them do so?

■ What record-keeping techniques did they use that you can adapt in your present job?

■ How did your more successful bosses handle employee grievances and morale problems? What can you learn from your experience with them?

■ What specific measures did they take to develop themselves and the people who worked for them? Which of these measures can you apply?

This isn't to imply, of course, that you should make yourself a clone or a composite of the best bosses you've had. Just the contrary. You bring your own unique personality, viewpoint, background, and experience to your new job, and given enough time and effort, you may become an even more effective manager than the best supervisor you've ever had.

Be prepared to employ your own methods, test your own ideas, and leave your own unique mark on your job and the organization. In addition, appreciate the fact that there's no "best" way to supervise people. Changing management styles, employee diversity, and new trends and developments in management thought combine to make you a pioneer of sorts. Your former supervisors may not have had the benefit of the tools, skills, talents, and information that you now have access to.

What Qualities Do People Respect Most in a Supervisor?

This question has no concise answer. One management professor and business writer asked hundreds of employees about the qualities they most respected in a boss; here are two dozen answers that he heard most often. Use them as a hip-pocket guide to help you succeed.

A good supervisor:

1. Keeps up-to-date on situations that affect future projects.

2. Maintains a positive attitude.

3. Has sound oral and written communications skills.

4. Explains actions and decisions that affect employees.

5. Doesn't play favorites.

6. Delegates authority and creates depth in management by allowing employees to do some of his or her job.

7. Is specific when giving instructions about delegated assignments.

8. Gives employees incentives to improve their job knowledge and efficiency.

9. Cross-trains employees so they can cover each other's absences.

10. Gives praise for work well done, and compliments as well as criticizes.

11. Is aware of problems that employees are having with each other.

12. Asks questions frequently, and is a concerned and active listener.

13. Organizes work schedules and assignments as effectively as possible.

14. Displays a professional attitude toward the work and employees.

15. Shows a human side; isn't compelled to act like "the boss" all the time.

16. Works with lower-level employees occasionally to understand what they do.

17. Takes time to listen to new ideas.

18. Pays attention to broader problems; avoids nit-picking.

19. Keeps people informed about changes.

20. Discusses problems with subordinates as soon as possible instead of letting things reach a boiling point.

21. Expresses feelings honestly.

22. Attempts to know each employee as an individual.

23. Uses new strategies that will make the organization more productive and competitive.

24. Shows confidence in subordinates.

Chapter 2

Manage Your Time

Managing your time effectively helps you prevent or minimize many problems and distractions that would otherwise interrupt your work. This chapter describes time management techniques that you should apply as soon as possible in your new job.

Organize Your Paperwork ASAP

Many new managers almost immediately either get bogged down in paperwork and ignore their team members or spend so much time with employees that they let their paperwork slide. One of the first things to do, then, is to develop some ground rules for handling the blizzard of paperwork that crosses your desk. More specifically, you need to:

■ Set guidelines for sorting, prioritizing, and answering all the mail that you receive.

■ Handle each document only once if possible. Don't let correspondence stack up. Robert Townsend, author of *Up the Organization* and the manager who made Avis one of the world's most successful auto-rental companies, liked to read his mail while standing over a wastebasket, which made it easier to discard marginal items. If something needed a reply, he wrote his answer on the original, made a copy for his files (but only if absolutely necessary), and sent it back to the originator. Townsend claimed he could answer several dozen letters during a morning with this approach.

■ Write standard or boilerplate phrases, sentences, and paragraphs that you can use in routine memos, letters, and reports. The time you invest now to develop this uniform correspondence will pay off impressively later. Instead of writing the same replies over and over, you can call up these prefabricated items on your personal computer (or retrieve them from a hard-copy file) whenever you need them.

■ Make charts, time lines, or other visual aids to track and display the deadlines and status of reports, projects, and rush jobs.

■ Categorize the regular correspondence you send and receive, and create a file folder for each category. Resist creating a "miscellaneous" file; it can grow into a monster. If you must have a general file, discard irrelevant items periodically and make new filing categories and folders for documents that should be filed separately.

■ Purge lengthy reports from your files as soon as possible to make room for new ones. Don't hoard old copies of updated reports or those that are obsolete.

These actions will keep your in-basket molehill from growing into a mountain.

Basic Time-Saving Tips

In addition to slaying the paperwork dragon, you can keep track of items that need future attention, minimize external interruptions, organize your physical work area, and account for how you use the hours in your day. Here are some techniques.

Keep a Bring-Up File

A bring-up file ensures that important items will surface again on the date when action is needed. "A bring-up file is one of the most valuable time-management suggestions I ever heard," says one business professor and freelance management writer. "I picked up the idea from John, an old-timer I worked with in my first management job. He had a collapsible file folder with pockets numbered from 1 through 31 in his bottom desk drawer, and he filed items that needed follow-up according to their action date. He checked his folder every morning for items he needed to work on that day. I never saw him overlook or misplace a single item in two years."

Organize Your Desk and Work Area for Maximum Efficiency

Place your file cabinets, wastebasket, reference books, and other frequently used items within arm's length, if possible. If you have a cubicle or office, position your desk out of sight of passersby to discourage idle conversation and drop-in visitors.

Use Your Computer Effectively

When it comes to managing time, your computer is your best ally. Make it earn its keep:

■ Save as much correspondence as possible on disk to reduce the space, equipment, and retrieval time consumed by hard-copy files.

■ Consider using color-coded disks for each project, and group them together so you can find the ones you're looking for at a glance.

■ Set up subdirectories on your hard drive for regular correspondence and projects so you can retrieve data without scrolling through dozens of general files.

■ Erase or archive unnecessary backup files or those that you haven't used for several weeks.

■ Defragment your hard drive periodically to maximize its efficiency and minimize wear and tear.

■ Record the phone and fax number and e-mail address of regular correspondents in your computerized address book. You can also insert these items as nonprinting comments in letters and memos so they'll be visible on the screen when you open a file.

■ Write and save macros for routine formatting operations such as page dating and numbering, setting margins, and inserting standard page headers and type fonts.

Keep a Time Log in a Pocket Notebook

A time log helps you analyze how and where you spend your time, and how it might be spent more efficiently. Note the nature of what you're doing every hour or two for several days so you can identify activities that eat up most of your time ("met with maintenance crew," "supervisors' meeting," "returned phone calls," "wrote/read correspondence," "set up overtime schedule," "rescheduled Owens job," "prepared budget," "ordered materials," etc.).

Examine and categorize the contents of this time log realistically by asking the following thirteen questions:

1. Is this a unique or one-time activity, or something that I have to deal with fairly often?

2. Could I do this task less often than I'm doing it now?

3. Which activities could I combine or consolidate somehow to save time?

4. Which tasks are interconnected or related in domino fashion, so that completing one of them automatically helps me finish other ones faster or more efficiently?

5. Which activities are so routine, simple, or by-the-book that they could be delegated to one or more people who report to me?

6. Which tasks should be done by a secretary?

7. How could this job be done faster without affecting its quality?

8. Which interruptions or crises could have been avoided or postponed until later in the day or week?

9. Could I have handled this job faster or easier using a different approach, such as a telephone call, e-mail, fax, or memo, or by simply referring to the policy manual?

10. Do I *really* have to do this chore, or am I doing it out of compulsion, force of habit, ritual, or an unwillingness to delegate?

11. Should this work be part of someone else's job description?

12. Am I using all the available technology (such as my personal computer and all of its existing programs and features) as effectively as possible to streamline and simplify each of these tasks?

13. Is this task so unlikely to come up again that I could disregard it?

Once you've categorized your most time-consuming tasks (which typically involve paperwork, meetings, scheduling, questions from subordinates, and filling out forms), pinpoint (1) those that you can do more efficiently, (2) those that should be delegated to the people who work for you, and (3) those that you can cluster together and work on all at once because they're complementary. For example, you can do both correspondence and telephone work at your desk, as opposed to tasks that require you to get out on the floor and meet with others.

It's up to you, of course, to overcome inertia. Nobody else can do it for you. Make a clean break with the obsolete or inefficient work practices you've identified by answering the above questions. It's possible that some of these activities have held you hostage for months or even years without your realizing it. It's time to acknowledge that now and improve your work practices.

Use Fragmented Time Productively

Fragmented time is the five or ten minutes you might spend waiting for a meeting to start or a new work shift to take over. Although it's tempting to disregard the value of these scattered chunks of time, minutes add up to hours, and hours add up to . . . well, you know the rest.

If you use these scraps of time productively, their total value can be impressive. Fragmented time can be good for such tasks as reflecting on current problems, mentally reviewing the status of rush jobs, editing a memo or report, or roughing out next week's work schedule.

Manage Your Open-Door Policy

Depending on the nature of your job, employees, and organization, an open door can be an invitation to chaos. Although you can't afford to be aloof or inaccessible, you may need to manage your accessibility if you want to get anything done.

There's no simple formula. Some managers like to set aside a specific time every day to meet with employees who need information or advice. Other managers have a "hideout," such as a vacant office or remote cubicle, that they can retreat to when they need to concentrate on an assignment without being interrupted. If neither of these ideas works for you, consider keeping your door partially closed (if you have an office) so people have to make a deliberate effort to interrupt you.

But what if you don't have an office? Make note of important information that people tell you so you can follow up later, after you've finished the task at hand. Also delegate as much authority as possible (more on this in Chapter 7) so subordinates can make routine, simple decisions without having to interrupt you. In addition, make it a habit to ask your employees to propose solutions to the problems they bring you instead of allowing them to dump their problems in your lap and run. Once word gets around that you expect to hear solutions as well as problems, your team members should be more prone to think for themselves before coming to you for advice.

Manage Your Telephone Time

If you usually have lots of calls to return, organize your day so you can return most or all of them at one sitting. If you need to stake out some quiet time, turn down the ringer or unplug the phone from the jack, if possible. Use voice mail to screen calls at your desk, and decide which ones you should take and which ones you'll return later.

You can also convert the phone into an asset, of course. Substitute a phone call and voice mail for face-to-face discussions with individual workers whenever possible, and use conference calls instead of summoning everyone together for face-to-face meetings.

Master Effective Reading Techniques

The avalanche of in-house correspondence and management articles and books you'll encounter demands that you hone your reading efficiency to a razor's edge. How can you stay abreast of all the reading that piles up in your in-basket? Here's a four-stage process recommended by Dr. Phyllis Mindell, based on her book *Power Reading*:

1. *Scan* the material and look for key words or phrases that relate to your job. If you find them or believe you need more information from the document, go back and skim it.

2. *Skim* (which is basically speed reading) the material to get the gist of the contents. Note the piece's structural or skeletal elements, such as the subject, title, subtitle, and subheadings. Skimming helps you decide which items are important enough to preread.

3. *Preread* the items that survived scanning and skimming by underlining key words and phrases in the text. Read precisely; in paraphrasing what the writer said, you will lose some of the original meaning. Pay special attention to the thesis statement or opening paragraph, the summary or conclusion, and each paragraph's topic sentence (which usually appears first). Few items—perhaps only one out of ten—deserve to advance to the fourth stage, which is deep reading.

4. *Deep-read* material by making margin notes, reflecting on the writer's message, searching for details, and decoding complex sentences. Read critically and skeptically; compare the writer's position with your own experience and the opinions other people have expressed on the subject. Jot down your agreements, disagreements, comparisons, and other reactions in the margin. Dissect the material as objectively as possible.

Chapter 3

Plan Your Day

Successful plans start with clear-cut goals; if you don't know where you're going, any road will take you there.

Goals answer the question, "What do I really want to do?" You must set your goals carefully because they will form the foundation for your plans. Managers who set goals and plan effectively have several key qualities:

■ They are comfortable sitting down with their employees as a team to discuss, clarify, and agree on goals.

■ They are patient when employees ask questions or act confused about what they're supposed to do.

■ They enjoy "selling" employees on the individual and group benefits they'll receive from helping their department carry out its plans and achieve its goals.

■ They are comfortable allowing employees to work without excessive supervision and direction, once goals have been set and plans are in place.

How can you tell whether your goals are sound? Look for the characteristics depicted in Figure 3-1.

■ *Realistic.* Goals should be achievable using your present resources (people, money, materials, equipment, and time). "Decreasing postage expenses 20 percent next year by printing our catalog on

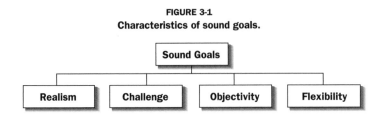

FIGURE 3-1
Characteristics of sound goals.

lightweight paper" is an example of a realistic goal because it could be accomplished without any additional resources.

■ *Challenging.* Although your goals must be realistic, they should also challenge your capabilities and those of the people who work for you. If not, you're all doomed to failure; if you don't grow, you die. Goals that require personal and organizational growth insulate everyone against mediocrity. No one ever found the route to success by maintaining the status quo. "Decreasing delivery expenses 15 percent by training drivers to plot their daily routes on laptop computers" might be considered a challenging goal.

■ *Objective.* Goals that are expressed objectively leave no doubt about whether they've been reached. Vague or subjective goals, on the other hand, make their achievement debatable and open to opinion. The most objective goals are expressed numerically because quantified goals are inherently objective. If you can't quantify a goal precisely, at least set a minimum target that you plan to hit—for example, "Our department's goal is to reduce customer complaints by at least 10 percent next quarter" or "We intend to cut rework and scrap by at least 15 percent this month."

■ *Flexible.* Be willing to revise your goals if unforeseen circumstances arise. For example, a change in competitors' strategies, economic conditions, supplies of available materials, or customers' buying habits might cause managers to revise their production and sales goals partway through a year. A salesperson who says, "I'll increase sales 12 percent in my territory next year if competitive and economic conditions don't change" has set a flexible goal. If conditions improve, the goal could be raised; if they worsen, it could be lowered.

Because your resources are limited and you can't do everything at once, it's likely that you'll have to prioritize your goals. When doing this, consider the following three guidelines:

1. Sort your goals into short-term and long-term categories. Give short-term goals that have a major impact on long-term goals a high priority. For example, if finishing short-term projects A, B, and C will make long-term program D easier or cheaper to complete, it makes sense to move projects A through C to the top of your priority list and throw your resources behind them.

2. Consider how your department's goals affect the goals of managers at your level and above. You'll want to give high priority to certain goals that, if not met, could pose problems for other departments or jeopardize the completion of a major project. The production line at one auto plant had to be shut down for almost an hour because employees ran out of left-hand taillights.

3. Take your boss's priorities into account. What does he or she need to accomplish and when? Modifying your priorities to support those of your boss reinforces your image as a team player and strengthens your relationship with him or her.

Involve Your Team Members

Make your employees stakeholders in your department's goals. Involving them in meeting the goals you set makes them more likely to support those goals as a team instead of as a collection of individuals.

Take, for instance, the retired executive who bought a donut shop. "I had $5,000 to spend on improvements," he said, "and it would have been easy to walk in and tell my employees what I thought we should buy. But I thought, 'Why not let them decide?' After all, they had to work there all day. So I told them how much I could afford to spend and said, 'Spend it however you want. Just make sure that what you do makes life easier, faster, or better for yourselves or our customers.'"

His workers grabbed the ball and ran with it. They found some excellent bargains in secondhand mixing equipment, had conveyor shutoff switches installed at various places around the room (previously there was only one), and suggested several economical and logical ways to improve drive-in service and spruce up the inside and outside of the building.

When you give your employees a vested interest in setting goals, they tend to work for themselves as well as for you. Enlightened self-interest can be a powerful motivator.

There will be times, however, when you'll set goals unilaterally. When that happens, ask yourself what factors or rewards you should emphasize to get your employees to back those goals 100 percent. For example, will reaching the goals improve working conditions? Give the people in your department greater job security? Make some tasks faster or easier to do? When you look at the benefits from your employees' standpoint, it's much easier to cultivate the stakeholder relationship mentioned above.

One way to adopt your employees' perspective is to ask yourself what benefits would have appealed to you before you became a supervisor. It can be just that simple. The same incentives that prompted you to support the goals of your former bosses are likely to appeal to the people who now work for you.

Types of Plans

The plans that help organizations achieve their goals fall into two general categories: single-use (or ad hoc) plans and standing plans. See Figure 3-2.

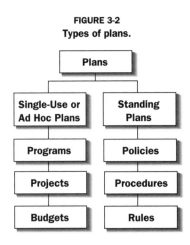

FIGURE 3-2
Types of plans.

Single-Use or Ad Hoc Plans

Plans created for a specific purpose are considered single-use plans and are discontinued after that purpose is reached. Single-use plans consist of programs, projects, and budgets.

■ *Programs.* Programs are created to achieve a general goal, such as reducing employee turnover, providing more job opportunities for minority applicants, converting traditional operations to teamwork, cross-training employees to perform multiple tasks, or improving employee morale. Because programs may exist for several years, they are often modified as time passes and business conditions change. For example, Pizza Hut allocated $100 million several years ago to convert the image and appearance of its restaurants from that of fast food to family dining.

■ *Projects.* Projects have more clearly defined goals than programs. For example, projects may be created to remodel existing facilities, reorganize the layout of a warehouse, develop a microchip that will increase a personal computer's speed by 300 percent, convert a manufacturing plant to just-in-time inventory management, or teach employees better ways to handle, store, and dispose of hazardous waste. When Zenith Electronics Corporation landed a billion-dollar contract to manufacture a new digital technology product, management created a highly motivational team compensation project to inspire members of the development team to deliver the product on or ahead of schedule. Teammates had the opportunity to earn up to $15,000 in bonus compensation for meeting all the milestones in the product's grueling schedule.

■ *Budgets.* Budgets are quantified projects that place an organization's goals in a numerical context. They have an exact life span (months, quarters, or a year, for example) and usually deal with money. It's also common, however, to create budgets for the number of employee-hours to be spent completing a given project, the amount of floor space to be reserved for specific departments or operations, and the amount of materials and supplies that may be allocated to making low-priority products in a manufacturing plant.

Standing Plans

Standing plans have no set lifetime; many of them live as long as the organization itself. Standing plans are generally classified as policies, procedures, and rules.

■ *Policies*. Policies are decisions made in advance. They're meant to answer popular questions in a uniform way whenever they arise. Policies serve as broad guidelines for behavior, and they're typically written down in a policy manual and (for more common policies) an employees' handbook as well. For example, Georgia-Pacific Corporation's manual on office conduct contains policies that deal with such issues as overtime, promotions, personal appearance, jury duty, lateness and absenteeism, outside employment, vacations, and equal employment opportunity, to mention just a few.

Policies reduce the likelihood that managers will be accused of behaving unfairly or arbitrarily. Top-level policies, which are stated in general terms, become more precise as they move down the management hierarchy to the supervisory level. A policy on reimbursing employees for business expenses might be interpreted as follows:

> TOP MANAGEMENT: "Authorized expenses in connection with company business will be reimbursed."
>
> MIDDLE MANAGEMENT: "Expense Reimbursement Form 122 lists reimbursable expenses and maximum limits if appropriate."
>
> SUPERVISORY MANAGEMENT (supervisor to employee): "When you go to the seminar in Tallahassee, Helen, the company will reimburse you up to $25 per day for meals, $60 per night for lodging, and $.25 per mile for travel in your personal vehicle. Fill out and sign Form 122 when you get back and give it to me. Be sure to attach all your receipts."

Interpreting policies can sometimes be frustrating because no two people may interpret written words exactly the same way. For this reason, policies are often revised to make them more clear. In addition, external influences—most notably laws and government regulators—will virtually dictate certain policies to management. For example, actions by the Equal Employment Opportunity Commission, passage of the Americans with Disabilities Act, and legislation prohibiting sexual harassment required management to create many policies that simply didn't exist—and may have been considered unnecessary—a number of years ago.

As mentioned above, lower-level managers are expected to interpret and apply policies and may sometimes have to ask for clarification. It's important not to criticize policies in the presence of your employees, however, no matter how strongly you may feel. Doing so can decrease morale and undermine higher management's leadership efforts. Supervisors who disagree with certain policies should make their feelings known through proper channels.

■ *Procedures.* Procedures are standing plans that list the steps for carrying out policies. In other words, policies tell *what* to do; procedures tell *how* to do it. The orderly, chronological sequence of procedures is meant to ensure that their related policies will be implemented in a logical and uniform way.

Most policies require procedures. The supervisor's last remark in the above example ("Fill out and sign Form 122 . . .") is actually a procedure because it tells the employee how to apply for her travel reimbursement.

One major insurance company's policy and procedure for dealing with employees who are convicted of driving while intoxicated on company business reads:

> POLICY: Employees are prohibited from using or being under the influence of alcohol or illicit drugs while operating a company-owned vehicle at any time or an employee-owned vehicle while driving on company business.
>
> PROCEDURE: A first conviction of driving under the influence in a company-owned vehicle at any time, or in an employee-owned vehicle being used for company business, will result in the following:
>
> ■ Use of the company-owned vehicle will be limited to company business (including driving to and from work) for a minimum of one year, at which time the circumstances will be reviewed.

- The employee's manager will thoroughly discuss the company policy on driving under the influence of alcohol or illicit drugs.

- The employee will be asked to complete an assessment for problem drinking or chemical dependency. If the assessment is positive and the employee agrees to treatment, he or she will be considered disabled and transferred to a position that does not require driving until he or she is released by the health-care provider to return to regular job duties. Employees who refuse assessment or prescribed treatment will remain employed only if there is a position available that does not require driving for company business. If the assessment is negative, the employee will be allowed to continue in his or her present job.

- An employee who has a second offense related to driving under the influence in a company-owned vehicle at any time, or in an employee-owned vehicle being used for company business, will be removed from the position that requires operating a vehicle. Continued employment will be subject to the availability of other positions for which the employee is qualified. If no positions are available, the employee will be terminated.

Procedures should be as simple as possible. Procedures that seem unnecessarily detailed aggravate and frustrate employees and encourage them to create shortcuts or bypass the "red tape" altogether. For example, one manager who wanted to requisition a longer phone line cord for his computer modem was disgusted with the formal procedure. It required him to fill out a form in triplicate, obtain approvals from two higher managers, and send it to the facilities department—which, he felt certain, would probably take two weeks to deliver the cord. He opted to go to Radio Shack and buy his own for less than $4.

- *Rules.* Rules are inflexible standing plans that usually prohibit or require specific behavior. They typically carry clear-cut penalties if they are violated. For example, employees may be discharged for smoking in a no-smoking area, engaging in horseplay, refusing to wear a hard hat on a construction site, being discourteous to customers, or falsifying information on time cards. Policies, by contrast, tend to be more flexible than rules.

Some companies with rules that require employees to speak only English at work have encountered problems because of today's cultural diversity in the workforce. An English-only rule may be permitted by the Equal Employment Opportunity Commission, however, if the employer can show that business must be conducted in English. Taco Bell permits discretion by stating that one language must be spoken in meetings and on production lines, but it does not specify which language.

Practical Principles of Planning

Goals are like the destinations on a road map. Plans are the routes you take to reach those destinations. Once you've decided what you want to do, it's time to develop plans to get you from where you are to where you want to be. There are four basic steps.

1. Start by assigning responsibility to the members of your team. Using their input where appropriate, decide what must be done, by whom, when, and how. You may have to clarify this both orally and in writing, depending on how complex the work is going to be. Hold follow-up meetings as necessary to answer questions and get feedback.

2. Give your people every opportunity to ask questions; don't assume they understand instructions the first time you give them. As you've probably heard elsewhere, "dumb questions are easier to handle than stupid mistakes." Once you've finalized the work assignments, give your employees enough authority to carry out their duties without interrupting you unnecessarily.

3. Emphasize the tangible group and individual benefits your plans are meant to produce. These might include, for example, reduced fatigue or effort; greater productivity; increased earnings; savings in cost, time, or materials; increased job security; and the satisfaction of belonging to a winning team.

4. As work proceeds, generate a spirit of competition and commitment among the members of your team by pointing out the recognition and success other departments or competitors have achieved from similar ventures. Knowing that others have blazed a trail assures your team members that they're not being asked to do the impossible or pursue results on paper that haven't been tested in the real world.

Of course, there's always the possibility that you may be involved in a pilot project or programs such as TQM (total quality management) or JIT (just-in-time) inventory management that your organization is implementing for the first time. If so, it's important to create a sense of esprit de corps, unity, and teamwork among employees (more on this in Chapter 5). People who have helped to set challenging goals and create the plans to carry them out will tend to invest their best efforts to ensure success.

Minimize Controls

Controls measure the pulse of progress, but don't let the tail wag the dog. Too much red tape (reports, status meetings, and other bureaucratic flak) strangles employees' initiative and creativity. Controls that become an end in themselves instead of a means to an end are a burden on everyone.

Controls tend to fall into three categories.

1. *Interdepartmental controls.* These might be company-wide or division budgets, meetings, reports, and financial statements.

2. *Intradepartmental controls.* These include departmental budgets, meetings, and reports; performance evaluations for employees who work within the department; and electromechanical quality assurance controls to monitor the operation of production equipment.

3. *Individual controls.* These may include employees' self-evaluations, personal procedures and rules they've devised to manage their own performance, and their individual sense of conscience, which may motivate highly responsible employees to do outstanding work whether or not they're closely supervised.

Give your employees as much freedom as possible to use their own initiative, employ their own methods, apply their own ingenuity, and monitor and report on their progress with minimal attention and direction from you.

What makes a sound control device? Ideal controls should be:

■ *Real-time based.* This means employees can identify and report problems ASAP. The difference between a minor glitch and a full-blown catastrophe often hinges on how much time goes by before somebody notices it. The best controls flag potential trouble before serious damage is done. Such is the case with numerical control devices that oversee and report the performance of automated production equipment. The space shuttle *Challenger*'s computers were the first to sense a problem with the mission. They responded by swiveling the engine nozzles around as far as possible, attempting to make an in-flight correction before the spacecraft exploded.

■ *Objective.* A control device is worthless if people can manipulate its output to make themselves look good. Objective control devices report identical results no matter who's using them. Budgets, go/no-go measuring gauges, and security systems that film shoplifters stealing merchandise on videotape are examples of highly objective controls.

Employee performance ratings that are based on vague standards or standards that managers may define however they wish suffer from a lack of objectivity. A sound evaluation system should at least describe the nature, extent, quality, and thoroughness of work that deserves to be rated "excellent" as compared to "good," "fair," or "needs to improve."

Supervisors who ask employees to rate themselves as part of the performance evaluation process must realize that people aren't likely to evaluate their own performance objectively. It's like someone who tells a friend, "According to the scales my weight is fine, but the chart says I'm six inches too short."

■ *Easy to understand.* If controls, such as status reports, approval forms, or quality-assurance equipment, are too complicated or confusing, people will avoid using them whenever possible.

■ *Cost-effective.* A control device should cost less than potential losses from the condition it's meant to monitor. For example, many fast-food restaurants now let customers pour their own soft drinks. Management found that the cost of having employees fill and serve each drink was greater than the losses from customers who helped themselves to free refills.

Managers in one company who were distressed by employee pilferage wanted to reduce theft by hiring more security guards. The salaries for the additional guards exceeded the cost of the inventory shrinkage, however. Management then decided to simply tell employees how this pilferage affected the company's profitability and therefore the value of the company's stock. Since most employees participated in the employee stock ownership plan, the pilferage rate dropped considerably after the announcement was made.

Report Progress With Visual Aids

Use line graphs, bar charts, time lines, or other graphics to track what's happening and serve as a rallying point for your employees' energy and commitment. In addition, visual aids will:

- Keep the team's collective efforts focused and unified.

- Give your group a sense of momentum and progress.

- Let everyone in your area confirm the status of major jobs whenever they wish (instead of having to attend a meeting or read a report).

Update visual aids often and whenever a significant change occurs.

Are You Ready?

Use the following five points as a preflight checklist for goals and plans:

1. Have you set and communicated clear goals?

2. Do the people who will carry out your plans understand and support the goals behind them?

3. Are your goals and plans compatible with those set by higher management and by other departments you work closely with?

4. Are your plans flexible enough to permit changes if circumstances require them?

5. Are your controls designed to monitor progress adequately without being too detailed or complicated?

Start Your Engines

If some of this information about planning seems a little abstract, relate it to a NASCAR race such as Talladega, Alabama, or the Daytona 500. All the members of a stock car team have one major goal: to win the race. To reach that overriding goal, however, the driver and pit crew must design a plan that takes into account the basic nature of the track, the car's handling characteristics, mechanical limitations, fuel consumption, probable weather conditions, the strategy of competing teams (based on previous races), the performance characteristics of competing cars, other drivers' personalities and previous behavior under pressure, and a host of other factors.

Next, the driver and crew chief must communicate their decisions to individual pit crew members and implement the plan by rehearsing such standard routines as refueling, changing tires, adjusting the car's suspension, and replacing minor parts until team members can perform their assigned tasks during pit stops that take no more than a few seconds.

Communications equipment in the car and inside the driver's helmet relays feedback about engine performance and the car's handling to the pit crew during the race. Dashboard gauges give the driver feedback on the engine's temperature, oil pressure, RPMs, and other vital signs during the race. The crew can change tires, adjust or replace suspension parts to alter the car's cornering and handling, and make other changes to respond to situations and problems that develop throughout the race.

Flexibility with equipment, personnel, and work assignments is vital. Each team must be prepared to compensate for many variables they'll encounter on race day. For example, teams must have several sets of tires, each with handling and track adhesion characteristics to suit anticipated race-day weather conditions, and spare parts (including at least one complete engine) because equipment may fail during qualifying runs. Crew members may be cross-trained to perform several different jobs in case someone on the team becomes ill or is injured in the pits.

All of these measures, and many more, are intended to lead to victory. In the context of supervision, this is a realistic example of how the elements of a successful plan must come together.

Chapter

4

Lead Your People

Effective leaders wear many hats. You'll be expected to serve as a role model for the people who work for you; coordinate their work; resolve their conflicts; promote their growth and development; represent them and your department to higher management and outside groups; and motivate them to achieve superior performance.

Good leaders aren't born. They develop and evolve through hard work, consistent effort, and an awareness of several factors that influence their success. Effective leaders:

■ Are comfortable taking charge, giving instructions, and acting assertively when necessary.

■ Work as collaborators, coaches, and colleagues with members of their group instead of feeling compelled to act like "the boss."

■ Focus on results more than methods. They let employees use their own judgment and employ their own approaches to carry out a task.

■ Don't breathe down people's necks. They're willing to supervise from a distance.

■ Acknowledge that employees usually have excellent ideas about how the work could be done better, faster, or cheaper and are willing to listen to those ideas at every opportunity.

Leadership Styles

Some authorities place leaders into one of four categories: autocratic, democratic, laissez-faire, and situational. It's important to realize, however, that there's no ideal approach to leading people. That will become clear as this section unfolds.

How do these four leaders differ from each other?

Autocratic leaders tend to be highly opinionated and militaristic. A consistent "I'm paid to think; you're paid to work" attitude rarely gets the best performance from employees, however, because most employees don't like to be treated like androids or interchangeable parts. Moreover, autocratic leaders deny themselves the input, suggestions, and viewpoints of their team members, which are often very helpful when figuring out how to solve a problem or tackle a new opportunity.

It wouldn't be right to say that you should *never* be an autocrat, though. For example, if you're training a totally inexperienced employee or dealing with unmotivated or indifferent employees, you may have to use an autocratic approach, at least temporarily. An autocratic leadership style may also be called for when employees must follow highly detailed, critical, or inflexible procedures such as those involved in assembling components that go into the space shuttle.

Democratic leaders, by contrast, see themselves and their employees as a team. Their slogan might be, "We're paid to think and work as a unit." Most people would rather work for democratic than autocratic leaders, and democratic supervisors tend to get the full benefit of their employees' ideas, opinions, and views. Supervisors who use this participatory, team-oriented style tend to need more time to solve problems or analyze opportunities, however, because they negotiate, discuss, and consult the employees as much as possible before making a decision.

Laissez-faire leaders provide general direction and overall guidance, but they give their employees as much freedom as possible. A laissez-faire boss might say, "Do this however you want, as long as you follow the rules." This hands-off leadership style may work well with highly trained, self-motivated persons who neither need nor want close supervision.

Distance may force some managers to be laissez-faire leaders, too. For example, if you're supervising people who work at several different locations or who travel a great deal, geography alone may dictate a free-rein approach. It would be physically impossible to stay on top of what each person is doing, all the time, every day. Employment decisions can be vitally important in these cases, of course. When distance is a factor, you must hire self-directed, mature people who can be trusted to manage their time, work schedules, and duties responsibly with minimal guidance from you. Laissez-faire supervisors tend to have a great deal of confidence in their employees' abilities and judgment.

Situational leaders adjust their behavior to the unique combination of factors that affect the situation at hand. These factors might be those depicted in Figure 4-1.

FIGURE 4-1
Factors that influence situational leadership.

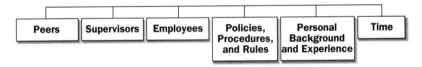

■ *Peers.* The dominant leadership methods of certain coworkers at your level may serve as a model for your own leadership actions, especially if you pattern yourself after your most respected and successful colleagues.

■ *Supervisors.* Managers who want to avoid philosophical or personality clashes with their supervisors may adopt a form of "protective coloring" by behaving like them. This may not be bad, of course, if these higher-level managers are effective leaders in their own right.

■ *Employees.* Employees' individual experience, training, skills, self-motivation, past and present performance, ambition, and work ethic can indicate which leadership approach (autocratic, democratic, or laissez-faire) may be called for in a particular situation.

■ *Policies, procedures, and rules.* These permit varying degrees of discretion in how managers may lead their team members.

■ *Personal background and experience.* Actions that have produced good results for you in the past are often worth repeating and making part of your regular leadership repertoire. Many successful managers have admitted to being influenced by former bosses, teachers, college professors, and parents whose ways of dealing with people and approaching challenging situations seemed to be especially effective. Likewise, effective leaders tend to avoid bad habits and practices that have caused ex-bosses, peer managers, or other people they've known to fail. As one successful manager said, "Nobody's ever useless—he can always serve as a bad example."

■ *Time.* You may not have enough time to deal with some situations the way you'd prefer. When time is too tight to allow for collaboration, a normally democratic manager may have to lead autocratically by making a unilateral decision.

Managers who adopt a situational leadership approach acknowledge the impact of these internal and external influences on each problem or task and adjust their response accordingly. By knowing their team members as individuals, supervisors can select the leadership approach that best suits the characteristics of the person at hand. In addition, successful supervisors adjust their leadership style to suit the particular situation.

Avoid Leadership Land Mines

Managers who have developed reputations as successful leaders didn't just luck into them. Part of their success can be credited to recognizing and avoiding several common pitfalls.

One obstacle to your success as a leader is the "stretch socks syndrome"—the belief that one size (or in this case, one leadership style) fits every person and situation. Not true. Managers who use only one approach for leading employees cannot get the best performance from everyone because individuals react differently to different leadership styles, and their reactions may be either positive or negative. Situational leaders realize this.

Another pitfall, one that's closely linked to the "stretch socks syndrome," is a new manager's tendency to be overly autocratic or dictatorial. Although an autocratic approach demands the least amount of effort and conscious thought, employees are generally excluded from the decision-making process except as tools to carry out what the boss thinks should be done. Managers who take it upon themselves to define problems and decide how to solve them sometimes run themselves out on a limb and end up sawing it off.

A third hazard to avoid is the tendency to adopt the same approach to leadership as one of your more impressive former managers used. The trouble with this is, you're leading an entirely different group of people under a different set of circumstances than your role model faced. It's important, then, to let your own technique evolve and take shape based on the nature of the people in your work group and the types of problems and challenges that your job presents. You can't—and shouldn't—be a clone of a previous boss, no matter how exceptional he or she might have been in your opinion.

Lead Different People Differently

The most outstanding leaders get to know employees as individuals and apply the leadership style that's most likely to get the best performance from each person. Modifying your leadership style to accommodate individual differences takes some focused effort on your part, but the payoff in superior performance is worth it. What qualities should you consider? Think about the person's previous experience, training, initiative, ambition, and apparent motivation. For example, you might give employees who possess a generous amount of those qualities minimal direction and control and relatively brief instructions when making assignments. A more autocratic approach might be called for if you're working with relatively new employees, those who lack self-confidence, or people whose past performance shows that they need detailed instructions and close supervision.

One management consultant recalled, "The most difficult question I was ever asked in a seminar was, 'How do I get my boss to lead me the way I want to be led?' This came from an employee who deserved and needed to be led democratically and worked for a boss who was an habitual autocrat. He wouldn't change his style for anyone or anything. The worker who talked with me was the best producer in the group, but her boss's leadership approach was killing her spirit. Every morning was a line-up-for-inspection and here-is-how-you'll-do-it affair. This treatment was so incompatible with her personality and competence that she was on the verge of resigning. The company was about to lose one of its best employees because of an inflexible leader.

"I frankly didn't know how to answer her question, but it certainly made me remember to tell every supervisor this: *Be willing to change your approach to accommodate your people.*"

Consider the Situation

Some situations, like some people, need to be led differently. For example, crises or nonnegotiable deadlines may require an autocratic approach. Someone has to step in, take charge, make decisions, allocate resources, assign responsibilities, and roll up his or her sleeves to ensure that the work gets done on time and right. If you're dealing with noncritical situations and/or routine tasks that are clearly covered by policies and procedures, however, you can afford to scale back to a more democratic or perhaps a laissez-faire approach. And guess what? Doing so makes you a situational leader.

Emphasize Results Over Methods

Some leaders are too prescriptive. They become obsessed with the techniques or approaches employees use to do the work instead of focusing on the results they're supposed to achieve.

The next time you make an assignment, try this: Tell the employees *what* you expect, then leave most or all of the decisions about *how* they should do it up to them. Sure this takes some courage, but the results might surprise you. When supervisors give employees the latitude to let their creativity flow, marvelous things can happen. When it comes right down to it, why should you care which methods employees use as long as the work gets done correctly, on time, within budget, and without violating policies and rules?

Supervisors who emphasize results over methods develop confident, competent team members who think for themselves and approach problems from several different angles. In other words, they empower and expect employees to think to the best of their abilities and employ their own resources all day, every day, for the benefit of everyone involved.

Keep in Touch With Your Troops

People respect leaders who physically come down to their level. Absentee managers who appear to be aloof or too busy, or who isolate themselves behind desks, walls, or secretaries, sometimes earn contempt from the rank-and-file.

You've got to see and be seen, and manage by walking around.

When you keep in touch with your troops, you have a superior sense of the rhythm and flow of the workplace. This practice is sometimes infinitely more valuable than relying on written reports and occasional comments from people who happen to drop by your desk. An added and obvious benefit, of course, is that employees will respect you for making the effort to get out and circulate among them and to listen to their comments, both positive and negative.

A textile company executive, recalling his days as a management trainee, had a supervisor who started out in one of the lowest-paid jobs in the company and rose up through the ranks to become a plant manager.

> I noticed during my first week that Mike walked through every department in the plant at least once a day. He called it his "plant tour." One day I asked him why he did it, especially when he had so many problems to sort out back in his office. He said it was the most important thing he did.
>
> "I want them to know I care—*really* care—about what's happening," he said. "When they see me face to face, it reinforces my sincerity and concern about all of us doing a good job. Oh, my supervisors keep me posted about lots of what goes on, but it's just not the same as seeing it first-hand. There's also the possibility that they might gloss over problems or try to keep a lid on them, hoping that they'll be able to put out the fire before I smell the smoke. But I don't want that, and I don't want our employees to think I'm too busy to stay in touch with what's really going on."

Your Role as Coach and Role Model

Effective leaders are inherently effective coaches. What makes them so are several key qualities:

■ They keep their employees' energy and efforts focused on clear goals that everyone understands and supports.

■ They generate and promote enthusiasm, self-confidence, and pride among their people.

■ They teach employees that frustration and failure can fuel a drive toward superior performance and success when the next set of opportunities arises.

■ They lead people to believe in and embrace the benefits that come from self-discipline, hard work, dedication to purpose, and a unified sense of direction.

■ They challenge and help employees to cultivate their individual skills to a razor's edge while channeling those skills toward goals that promote the success and reputation of the team as well as its members.

Effective leaders also appreciate their impact as role models. They realize they can set performance and behavior standards by default as well as by design. Some of the most important areas where you can exert a positive influence are:

■ *Customer service.* Dedicate yourself to meeting commitments to internal and external customers fully and on time. Resolve problems, complaints, and questions promptly and cheerfully. Speak of customers with respect. Managers who bad-mouth them give tacit approval for employees to do the same.

■ *Policies.* Confirm by your actions that you hold yourself to the same standards that you expect from employees. Don't ignore policies that don't suit your purpose or spread dissatisfaction by griping about them to employees. Take your complaints to higher management.

■ *Ethical conduct.* Acknowledge your organization's code of ethics throughout the hiring and orientation process. Affirm your commitment to it in meetings, personal conversations, and written documents.

■ *Behavior in a crisis.* Panic is both unbecoming and contagious. When emergencies arise, keep your composure. This speaks well for you and helps to keep the people around you calm, too.

■ *General work habits.* Work habits include such basic conduct as arriving at work and returning from lunch promptly, working late when necessary, meeting deadlines, and managing your behavior and your job with utmost professionalism. Supervisors who demand the best behavior from themselves can justify demanding the same from their employees without appearing hypocritical or unreasonable.

Leading a Diverse Workforce

Today's workplace, like society itself, is more like a tossed salad than a melting pot. Diversity has always existed among employees, but now it's being recognized, encouraged, and valued in more ways than ever before.

Types of Diversity

The concept of diversity as it is applied to a work group has no universal meaning. Although people differ from one another in many ways, their differences revolve around individual and cultural traits.

Individual Diversity

Many individual traits or characteristics make an employee unique. These include (but certainly aren't limited to) age, sex, and ethnic background; physical and mental abilities; self-concept; education; marital status; personality; how quickly he or she learns new information; the length of time he or she has worked for the organization; and how long he or she has been in his or her present job.

Cultural Diversity

Employees differ from each other culturally on the basis of their native language, religion, social class, and the customs, habits, and values that are part of their culture. For example, Asian Indians may be reluctant to speak frankly to supervisors because relations with elders and superiors are relatively restricted in India. Asians and Nigerians avoid eye contact as a sign of respect and courtesy, while Africans and the British may break eye contact and turn their heads to concentrate on listening. Asians, who dislike confronting coworkers and contradicting elders, may not disagree with a supervisor's idea, no matter how outrageous it might be. Hispanics, on the other hand, may feel that contradicting the boss is not disrespectful and may speak more candidly in meetings than employees from other cultures. Hispanic supervisors may start a meeting with small talk instead of getting down to business because of their cultural tendency to view the work group as a close-knit family.

Why Value Diversity?

Supervisors have a host of sound reasons for valuing diversity.

■ Employee turnover is lower in organizations that welcome a diverse workforce. Employees appreciate working for enlightened employers, and this appreciation is reflected in their reluctance to quit and seek employment elsewhere.

■ Organizations that value diversity cultivate a sound reputation as socially conscious, responsible, and responsive employers. They are seen as a good place to work and a positive force in their communities and industries.

■ Managers who encourage and support a diverse workforce create and maintain high employee morale and its two major by-products: greater productivity and profitability.

■ Valuing diversity promotes honest, candid communication among all members of the organization and gives employees a sense of value, self-respect, and belonging.

■ Organizations that value diversity enable all employees to develop, grow, and achieve their true potential through enhanced skills and promotional opportunities.

■ Encouraging diversity brings greater creativity and objectivity into the decision-making process. Such qualities may not exist in homogeneous "cookie cutter" organizations where management implies, by words and actions, that everyone should look, think, and act as if he or she came from the same mold.

Norrell Services set the following goals for the Corporate Diversity Strategic Plan that it implemented in the mid-1990s:

1. Reduce turnover.

2. Grant recognition based on true contribution.

3. Seek a balanced family and work life.

4. Encourage competent, caring, confident management.

5. Develop diversity at all levels.

6. Recognize valued differences among employees.

7. Seek to have half of the workforce remain with the company for five years.

8. Get stock to reach $40 per share.

9. Increase morale.

10. Ensure that company opportunities exist for everyone.

11. Achieve less nit-picking.

12. Try to encourage a caring company.

13. Develop more knowledgeable employees.

14. Encourage candid communication.

15. Give employees greater opportunities for personal growth.

16. Seek to have the company viewed as a preferred employer in and out of its industry.

Norrell's goals reflected many benefits of encouraging and fostering diversity in the workplace. Diverse employees offer a rich blend of viewpoints, skills, talents, and perspectives. These qualities reflect those of society at large and the many different internal and external "publics" that an organization serves or is accountable to.

Proving Your Sincerity

Organizations and supervisors who value diversity prove their sincerity in several ways.

- Policies and procedures are written to help diverse groups succeed, advance, and feel respected and important.

- Supervisors understand and are responsive to the needs of diverse groups.

- Supervisors actively and sincerely seek and acknowledge contributions and opinions from all employees.

- All employees have equal access to organizational resources that can help them succeed.

- Employees are made to feel valued and accepted regardless of their individual or cultural diversity.

Promoting Acceptance of Diversity

Organizations and supervisors can take several positive measures to promote acceptance of and appreciation for diversity. Although some of these actions must originate with or be carried out by top management, others fall within the reach of individual supervisors.

Forward-looking organizations provide diversity awareness and sensitivity training to managers at all levels. Since the late 1980s, for example, ARCO chemical company has hired consultants to teach courses in managing workforce diversity. This effort was an important factor in recruiting foreign-born employees both in the United States and abroad. ARCO's Corporate Equal Opportunity Affairs manager said, "We need to educate our people so we can recruit and retain the best."

Higher management also promotes acceptance of diversity by acknowledging and including diversity goals in supervisors' performance evaluations and incentive compensation. In addition, supervisors must be responsible for emphasizing the organization's position on and respect for diversity as outlined in the employee handbook and discussed during new employee orientation sessions.

Managers at all levels can provide organizational activities that include members of all individual and cultural groups. When The St. Paul Companies took the initiative to manage diversity in 1992, higher management formed a Managing Diversity Committee and subcommittees to acknowledge the special needs and interests of the disabled, minorities, gay men and lesbians, and women. Employees who became active on these committees were invited to meet with The St. Paul's top executives over dinner to exchange views and concerns in an informal diversity awareness session. Afterward, executives agreed to have regular sessions to deal with interpersonal work issues and confront personal biases. They also created awareness programs for managers and officers and increased communications that addressed managing a diverse workforce.

Improving Your Personal Cultural Awareness

How can you improve your own cultural awareness? San Francisco diversity consultant Lewis Griggs, the author of *Valuing Diversity*, offers these four suggestions:

1. Pay attention to how you act. Notice how you speak and the messages you send with your body language when you talk to people of higher and lower status.

2. Learn about other employees' cultures. Read magazines, attend cultural events, and go to the churches of different cultures. The more you know, the more understanding and tolerant you become.

3. Adjust. Accept others' differences instead of expecting them to be more like you.

4. Value the cultural differences that your employees bring to their jobs. Take advantage of traits that can help you, your team, or your entire organization achieve its goals more effectively.

The Norrell Services plan referred to earlier was the brainchild of a fourteen-member Diversity Council whose goal was "To be the change agents that develop a Corporate Diversity Strategic Plan that meets the challenges and capitalizes on the opportunities of a diverse workforce." The council set six objectives:

1. Develop a diversity vision statement.

2. Set goals to eliminate artificial barriers that might hinder the hiring and advancement of diverse members of the corporation into management and other higher-level positions.

3. Provide recommendations for policy changes.

4. Develop an education process for all members of the corpo-

ration to foster understanding and help eliminate bias in the workplace.

5. Develop a five-year implementation strategy.

6. Develop a communication plan.

Less than one year later, after developing the above objectives, the council conducted focus group meetings and held surveys to define the company's critical issues, create company-wide diversity objectives, develop strategies and tactics for achieving those objectives, and communicate the council's goals to employees at all levels by internal company publications and managers' meetings.

Chapter 5

Build Your Team

The use of teamwork in today's organizations has advanced far beyond a trend; it's a full-blown revolution that has changed how work is organized, assigned, performed, and supervised. For example:

■ General Electric has built its entire organization around the concept of self-managing work teams. Employees at one team-based G.E. plant in North Carolina are 250 percent more productive than other plants that make the same products. Workers can switch production among more than ten different models a day.

■ A General Foods plant in Topeka, Kansas, that's specifically designed for team-based work is 30 percent more productive, is cheaper to operate, and has higher employee morale than other plants.

■ For more than twenty years, Motorola has credited teamwork with reducing turnover by 25 percent, increasing productivity more than 30 percent, and raising attendance 95 percent.

■ Many companies routinely use cross-functional teams of research and development, production, and marketing employees to guide products all the way from inception through development, production, and marketing.

Why Use Teams?

Many organizations have jumped on the teamwork bandwagon because teams can assemble and apply members' skills, experience, viewpoints, and strengths to achieve superior results compared to how well individuals produce by working alone. In addition, teamwork can encourage employees to be more committed to success, feel a greater sense of purpose in and contribution to their work, become more involved in their organization's goals and plans, exchange more ideas for improving systems and procedures, contribute more solutions to problems, and take advantage of opportunities more effectively.

Work teams increase unity and a sense of purpose among employees. In addition, you'll spend less time directing traffic, making assignments, and arbitrating disagreements among employees who work as semiautonomous units. Teamwork also gives your group a greater sense of identity and a collective, contagious pride in its performance. People feel gratified and rewarded when they're members of a winning team.

How Can You Use Teams?

There are several practical ways to apply teamwork principles in a group or department setting. See Figure 5-1.

FIGURE 5-1
Ways to apply teamwork.

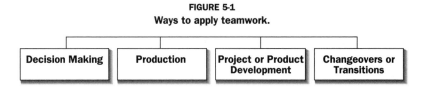

■ *Decision making.* As a manager, you can use teams to gather, analyze, and summarize information about problems or opportunities. You can also make a team responsible for recommending potential solutions to problems based on information the team has assembled. Or, to take the ultimate step, you could empower a team to actually decide certain issues as a group and implement its decision.

You can use decision-making teams to resolve production bottlenecks, improve customer service, streamline paperwork flow or work layout, or reduce machine downtime for preventive maintenance or model changeovers.

■ *Production*. Production teams have long been used by such companies as Saab and Volvo. Work permitting, team members may be cross-trained to do a variety of tasks, which maximizes flexibility, minimizes boredom, and may increase employees' job security. Cross-training may not be practical, however, if tasks are highly specialized (such as the work of space shuttle teams and race car pit crews).

■ *Project or product development*. Team members may join forces to reduce the time needed to develop and test prototypes or bring a new model to market. In such cases members are usually drawn from the marketing, design, engineering, manufacturing, purchasing, and finance departments. For example, managers at Ford Motor Company created such cross-functional "world-class timing" teams to develop new models of the Probe, Thunderbird, and Mustang. Team members worked together at the same location and reported to one project manager instead of to the managers of their individual functions.

■ *Changeovers or transitions*. Teams may also be assembled to coordinate the efforts of various departments that must work together to install new systems, procedures, or equipment. In such cases the team serves as a steering committee to oversee the direction and implementation of the change.

Work Teams: Some Basic Guidelines

Work teams succeed and flourish because both managers and team members work hard and pull together. Here are nine guidelines to help you build and work through teams.

1. *Set goals as a team.* This collective approach helps to ensure that everyone accepts and supports what the group sets out to do. People feel a stake in and a personal commitment to goals they've had a hand in setting. Make sure the team defines its goals clearly and quantifies these goals wherever possible (a point made in Chapter 3). The more precise the goal, the better team members can monitor and assess progress as they focus their energy and resources on reaching it.

2. *Reward group performance over individual performance.* Group rewards encourage team members to police each other's work. In addition, such rewards build members' loyalty to the team and motivate each member not to be the weak link in the chain. Group rewards also motivate team members to be mutually supportive, rally behind each other's efforts, and unite to eliminate problems that may jeopardize the group's success.

Your group reward system must also include frequent feedback on the team's performance, so members can monitor their collective progress. This enables them to take fast action when things go haywire. An eye-catching chart, graph, or other visual aid often fills the bill.

Group rewards are limited only by your ingenuity and budget. They may include, for example, public praise, a bonus to be shared among team members, a rotating trophy that's temporarily "owned" by the best-performing team, or assignment to a more desirable work shift or project.

3. *Cross-train team members whenever feasible.* Cross-training permits members to trade off responsibilities, and that alleviates boredom and monotony. You may also find that workers become so proficient that you can let them distribute certain tasks among themselves or decide which jobs each one will do during a shift.

4. *Become a sounding board, constructive critic, and advisor.* This is a hard adjustment for some managers to make, but it's absolutely vital to the success of the team. Supervisors must accept the idea that they're no longer "the boss" in the traditional sense. Organizations that apply teamwork successfully have transformed managers into facilitators who ensure that each work team has all the information and resources it needs to do its job. The supervisor no longer controls the group because *everyone* becomes responsible for results. In teamwork, a manager is a guide on the side, not a sage on the stage. Some team-oriented companies allow teams to elect their own leaders from among the ranks and even to rotate the job of leader periodically.

5. *Don't let teams become isolated from each other.* Make sure that they coordinate and synchronize their efforts with other key parties and groups inside and outside your department that may depend on them for input, output, or information. In other words, a sense of unity must not only infect the members of a given team but also spread among the teams themselves. Their collective and mutually supportive efforts affect the entire organization.

6. *Keep team membership relatively small.* There are several advantages to building small work teams. Small teams pose fewer coordination and communication problems; managers find it easier to reach agreement and consensus among members of a small group; and members of small groups tend to bond more closely than members of large groups (which often form factions and splinter groups within themselves). You may want to promote a team identity through badges, caps, jackets, patches, decals, or other insignia that encourage cohesiveness and a feeling of combined purpose.

7. *Select members who have both complementary and counterbalancing views and skills.* This may mean, for example, that you would deliberately combine positive thinkers and skeptics, free-thinking innovators and regimented pragmatists, and dreamers and doers. Such a mix gives the team an internal system of checks and balances on its members' actions and decisions.

8. *Walk your talk.* How you talk around your team reveals whether you've really embraced teamwork in your own mind. Although the difference in words may be subtle, it reflects where you're really coming from. For example:

Don't Say	Do Say
I	We
Your	Our
What's the problem?	Let's find out what's wrong.
What do you need?	What do we need?
What are you going to do about it?	What should we do about it?
Can I help?	How can I help?
Who's responsible for this?	How can we fix it?
You're doing it wrong.	How about trying it this way?
This isn't good enough.	We have to do better.
I don't believe you should . . .	Why don't we try . . .

9. *Be patient.* It may take two years or even longer for a work team to galvanize into a cohesive, productive, self-directed unit. After all, teamwork is a fundamental shift in organizational tradition, philosophy, and culture. Success won't happen overnight.

Needed: Some Form of Training

Throw a bunch of individuals together haphazardly, and you may get nothing but collective chaos. Be alert to a team's need for training in such areas as:

- Using the decision-making process

- Avoiding "groupthink" (the tendency for some members to defer to the majority or certain opinion leaders instead of challenging their assumptions or position)

- Acknowledging and respecting opposing viewpoints (disagreeing without being disagreeable)

- Accepting differences in each other's ethnic background, work experience, personalities, and other factors that may distract some members from the team's collective mission

Leading Team Meetings

The very nature of teamwork demands that your teammates meet often to discuss, decide, or simply exchange opinions and information. Several guidelines can help you lead these meetings effectively and advance the spirit of teamwork in the process.

Don't

■ *Make all the arrangements yourself.* It's your *team's* meeting. Let the members decide what they want to discuss, where to meet, and when. Rotate the chair and any other official duties among all the members so everyone has a turn. Avoid the chair at the head of the table; it's the traditional authority position. If no one else takes it, leave it vacant. That sends a positive message about how you view your role.

■ *Pass judgment or comment on members' remarks and ideas.* Acting like an expert or critic destroys team spirit, inhibits discussion, and shows that you still see yourself as an authority figure instead of a facilitator. Withhold your opinion (count to 10 or bite your tongue if necessary) to show team members that you're not going to judge the quality of their input.

In one fledgling team meeting, a new employee innocently suggested an operation that his department's equipment couldn't do. "That's ridiculous!" the old-line supervisor blurted. "Our machines won't operate that way. Haven't you been around long enough to know that?" The new guy turned beet-red, hung his head, and never spoke a single word in future meetings.

■ *Act like you have all the answers.* Teams collaborate on problems and produce consensus solutions. You may coordinate, facilitate, and participate, but don't behave like an expert. You already have a collective expert: your team.

■ *Be confrontational.* Demanding that people defend their ideas and opinions when they conflict with yours reveals an autocratic "I'm paid to think/you're paid to work" mind-set. That's the antithesis of teamwork.

■ *Use the same meeting management techniques as your former supervisors in traditional organizations.* New roles call for new techniques. Old ways won't work in team-oriented organizations.

■ *Feel compelled to assert or maintain control over the meeting.* Surviving in a team-based organization means accepting and operating with greatly diminished control. That requires you to change mental gears and adopt an entirely new perspective. If you've worked in traditional organizations, you'll have to do some hard mental labor, soul-searching, and self-analysis. No one said it would be easy.

■ *Let team members pass the buck to you.* Refuse to play the role of supreme commander or resolve issues that are best left to your team. One four-person team, deadlocked on an issue of work assignments, asked the leader to arbitrate the dispute. He agreed to meet with them and asked them to choose the time and location. After they sat down, he said, "Since we're a team, I'm not comfortable making this decision for you. First of all, have you agreed that you want to agree?"

They nodded. "Good. Then I think I should take myself out of the picture and leave the decision to you. I'll help in any way possible, but this is *your* work, and *you* should make the call. Just let me know what you decide, okay?" With that he excused himself and left them to work it out—which they did.

Do

■ *Prepare for the meeting.* Make notes, review and reflect on the team-produced agenda, gather important materials, reserve a room if necessary, and requisition and test-run any audiovisual equipment.

■ *Think of yourself as a participant, coordinator, and general guide.* You may have to arrange for the room and equipment, but it's not your job to "call a meeting" or "run it" in the traditional sense. Once it starts, descend to everyone else's level—and stay there.

■ *Encourage devil's advocates.* People who have the courage to swim against the current by questioning, challenging, or contradicting the majority are very valuable to a team. They strike a blow against groupthink. That state of mind can be disastrous because it causes team members to avoid self-censorship, refuse to question each other's beliefs, refrain from speaking their opinions (for fear of being ostracized for having opposing views), and ignore important information in the quest to preserve consensus and avoid conflict. Don't play devil's advocate yourself, however, for reasons mentioned earlier.

■ *Use visual aids that dramatize group progress and performance.* These depict collective success and generate a sense of unity. Let team members themselves develop and update these materials before each meeting, and have them take turns presenting and summarizing what they show.

■ *Draw people out.* Begin with open-ended prompting remarks such as "How do you feel about . . ." "Tell us more," or "We all need to hear what you think." Getting people to open up is especially important when you suspect they have more to say or aren't sharing their true feelings.

■ *Tape-record the discussion.* Analyze your conduct and comments. See if you're coming across to your people the way a true team leader should, and earmark areas for improvement.

■ *Provide closure.* The meeting should leave members with a sense of accomplishment. You might ask, "What have we decided to do?" but let team members confirm closure by summarizing who's responsible for what, when it's to be done, and which subjects should be carried forward to the next meeting.

■ *Summarize your thoughts and impressions in writing after each meeting.* Use this information, along with your audiotape, to identify which aspects of the meeting went smoothly, which ones did not, what things you might do differently next time, and which of the above do's and don'ts you should pay more attention to when the next meeting comes around.

Gaining Team Consensus

Although they usually take longer to reach, consensus decisions typically receive more support because team members have all their oars in the water and are pulling in the same direction.

Team members need the proper collective mind-set for making consensus decisions. Although this may take some time, the more effort that you invest at the beginning of the process (confirming group readiness and resolving potential obstacles to agreement), the more time you'll save on implementation because team members will have agreed on their plan of attack. Here are five questions to help you assess your team's readiness to reach a consensus:

1. Will all team members be active and voluntary participants? (Members who conceal their true opinions or have hidden agendas can frustrate the process or produce a false consensus.)

2. Do team members clearly understand the key issues and concerns behind each of the tasks involved? (If in doubt, you might propose a preliminary question-and-answer session to help them grasp the importance of each item they'll be asked to examine so they can set rational priorities.)

3. Are they aware of all the circumstances and conditions that should influence their determination of priorities? (For example, they may not understand the relative urgency of some tasks or realize how much time, budget money, or other resources they have at their disposal.)

4. Will they be willing to reach a consensus on how to attack these various jobs? (Before pursuing a consensus, it's important for group members to agree that they want to agree! That's the foundation for everything that follows.)

5. Are they willing to let the team's, department's, and higher management's concerns override any personal agendas?

If you can honestly answer yes to the above questions, here are several group decision-making techniques that can help move the team toward agreement.

■ If your team is fairly small, you might start by having each person prioritize the tasks privately, then present and justify those priorities to the group. This process may reveal interesting and relevant information some members were unaware of that may influence their opinions. After this you might consider using one or more of the following practices.

■ Do a cost/benefit analysis to identify tasks that will give the team or your organization the greatest payback for the cost (in time, materials, and other relevant factors) expended. Team members must also acknowledge the relationships among various tasks. For example, some may run sequentially or be interdependent (that is, you may have to complete jobs A, B, and C before you can start or fully complete job D).

■ Prepare a "Ben Franklin balance sheet." The group could write down the name of each project on a separate sheet of paper, then list the reasons for completing it ASAP on one side and the reasons for postponing it on the other side. Next, they would weight the reasons on a scale of 1 to 5 (which, admittedly, may prompt considerable debate), add up the scores, divide by the number of reasons, and see which side—pro or con—has the highest average score.

At the very least this technique may help your team achieve consensus on jobs that demand immediate attention. Those with the highest scores on the ASAP side might be prioritized according to their relative scores.

■ Split the team into two groups. Have each group prioritize the tasks on paper, then get back together to compare results. Jobs that received the same priority from each group are no longer an issue.

Repeat the process with tasks about which they disagreed. During the final meeting, consider taking a vote on projects that neither side could reach consensus about. This at least shows how strongly members feel about each one.

■ If the team is deadlocked on a priority rating for certain tasks, members might split into two groups (pro and con), present their respective arguments, and try for consensus once more. If that fails, perhaps cost/benefit analysis might be employed as a tie-breaker.

It's important for you to stick to your role as facilitator throughout this process. Although your team may be frustrated in its efforts to reach agreement, staying on the sidelines and resisting members' appeals to become an arbitrator ensures that you won't taint the spirit of consensus that the group needs to give the final priority list its wholehearted support.

Hire Team-Oriented Employees

Successful teamwork actually begins with hiring. Select applicants whose background, experience, and work habits are compatible with the tenets of teamwork. (Note: Hiring and orientation are discussed in more detail in Chapter 8.) Here are four techniques to help you gauge applicants' potential as team members before you call them in for an interview.

1. Evaluate their extracurricular activities, work experience, and former job responsibilities from a team perspective. Which candidates participated in team sports and clubs, held elected offices, or did volunteer work that required them to coordinate activities and cooperate with others? What jobs did they have (and for how long) that helped them develop the ability to interact with and support the efforts of coworkers?

2. Contact former supervisors, club sponsors, teachers, and other references. Although the law limits how candidly these people may speak, read between the lines of their remarks for clues about the applicants' ability to relate to colleagues.

3. Ask ex-bosses to discuss the applicants' former job responsibilities and how they may have prepared the applicants to work well on a team.

4. Consider allowing present team members to participate in the hiring interview. Doing so will require you to train them in proper interview technique, of course, including potential legal problems that may arise from discussing topics that aren't related to BFOQ's (bona fide occupational qualifications). Doing team interviews may be well worth the time and effort, however, because members will gain a greater sense of participation in—and bring more objectivity to—the hiring process. Who is better qualified to assess an applicant's suitability for joining a team than the members themselves?

Whether you involve team members or not, be sure to use the employment interview to confirm the impressions you got from former supervisors and other outside parties. In addition, assess applicants' team orientation and temperament by asking them such questions as:

- Would you summarize the most memorable challenge you faced in a previous job and tell me how you dealt with it?

- What approach would you take to resolve a disagreement or personality conflict with a coworker?

- How do you feel about sharing credit for what you've done with other people in your work group?

- How do you feel about working in a group where everyone depends on you and you depend on them?

Once you've made your selection, use orientation to infuse new employees with "how business is done" in your team-based organization. More specifically:

- Review the job description. Although you may (and likely should) discuss the job description with applicants during the employment interview, orientation gives you another chance to stress the job's team-related duties and responsibilities.

- Flowchart responsibilities both within and among work teams. A flowchart illustrates and dramatizes key links among team members and the teams themselves. When properly presented, it leaves no doubt that you expect mutual support, cooperation, and an "all for one and one for all" attitude.

■ Use existing team members in orientation. Peer pressure can be an impressive motivator. Presentations by existing team members who have bonded and work well together can make a lasting impression on new employees.

■ Consider a rotating orientation program that involves each team member. Teammates have a vested interest in each new member's performance. Having them describe and demonstrate their responsibilities with new hires one-on-one drives home not only what they do but also why it's important and how it contributes to the entire team's success. At the conclusion, members could meet as a group with the new employees to display unity, answer questions, summarize their roles, and provide additional information about their collective responsibilities.

■ Talk your walk. As mentioned earlier, make sure that your vocabulary confirms and reinforces your personal and professional dedication to teamwork throughout the hiring and orientation process. Saying "we," "us," and "our" (instead of "I," "me," and "mine") verifies your commitment in fact as well as spirit.

Teamwork Isn't for Everyone

You might find that some of your present employees aren't temperamentally suited for team membership and group efforts, despite whatever training or other measures you've applied. If that happens, you may need to transfer them to more traditional departments or tasks where their lone-wolf tendencies won't impede (and may actually enhance) their success.

In extreme situations, however, an employee may be openly and totally hostile to the idea of working as a member of a team or sharing group rewards. If that's the case, and if you've exhausted all efforts to find a suitable position that accommodates the person's skills and abilities, you may have little choice except discharge.

Chapter

Make Effective Decisions

Decisions become the landmarks of every manager's career. What you do about the problems and opportunities you meet in your job has a cumulative and often a comprehensive impact on your reputation and success.

Effective decision makers:

- Solicit and weigh information and opinions from many sources.

- Listen to and respect other people's views even if those views conflict with their own.

- Are willing to modify or discard a decision that proves to be defective.

- Share credit generously with everyone involved in a successful decision.

- Don't place blame or criticize people in front of others.

- Refuse to be pressured. They'll fight for enough time to gather necessary information and investigate the matter thoroughly.

- Realize that unforeseen conditions will cause some decisions to turn out bad no matter how carefully they were made.

- Put past mistakes and bad decisions behind them and move forward with a positive outlook.

Types of Decisions

Managers make two general kinds of decisions. The first, a *problem decision*, is a decision that's made to resolve some difficulty that poses a real or potential threat to progress. Problem decisions may be broken down into *ad hoc decisions*, which are made to deal with problems that aren't likely to happen again, and *programmed decisions*, which are decisions based on precedents or policies that tell managers how to deal with routine problems. Programmed decisions are the easiest ones to make. They ensure that managers resolve recurring problems or questions consistently each time they arise.

Your work as a manager will also require you to make *opportunity decisions*, which are made either to take advantage of or to reject opportunities that may help you achieve your goals. Decisions to purchase new equipment or overhaul existing machines, change from one long-distance communications company to another, and accept a promotion as head of a new department would be opportunity decisions.

Opportunity decisions are often made in conjunction with planning, which you learned about in Chapter 3. They require managers to evaluate circumstances, assess available resources (people, time, money, space, and equipment), and decide whether to keep on doing business as usual or strike out in a new direction.

Although this chapter focuses mainly on problem-oriented decisions, remember that the eight-step process you'll learn can also be applied, with few changes and equal success, when you're deciding whether and how to cash in on certain opportunities you'll encounter from time to time.

Ask the Right Questions First

Managers who set aside time to ask thoughtful and probing questions at the outset improve their odds of making good decisions. Talk to employees who are closest to the problem. You'll gather more information, have a better perspective, and be able to act more confidently than if you relied solely on your own resources, opinions, and perceptions.

Your employees often know more about a problem than you do, but you may never discover that unless you ask them. Don't expect employees to volunteer opinions without being encouraged. Some employees may underestimate the value of their views, while others may believe you don't want to hear what they think.

Besides getting fresh and often valuable insights, asking employees for their opinions demonstrates your commitment to being a democratic leader. Moreover, getting others' opinions helps you avoid making a solo—and perhaps incorrect—decision.

When you want your employees to participate in a decision, avoid calling them into your office. People are often more comfortable when you meet them on their own turf. Talking to them behind their own desks or in their own work area puts them at ease; they'll tend to speak more freely.

Talk to your employees one-on-one first. Some workers will keep silent in a group, fearing that their coworkers might criticize or make fun of them. When you talk to them individually, however, they're more likely to speak candidly about the problem and how they think it might be solved. In any case, assure your employees that you'll keep their comments confidential if they wish.

You may want to hold a group session after you've talked to employees individually. Here you can lay some of their ideas about the problem on the table and get collective feedback. Group discussion also gives your employees an opportunity to modify and combine their ideas in very creative and useful ways. At the very least, hearing the group's response improves everyone's objectivity.

Play the role of collaborator. Make employees feel like they're part of a team. It's important to be nonjudgmental about *everything* at this point because people will clam up if you're too negative or critical. ("Why should we tell him anything? He's already got all the answers.")

An open-minded attitude encourages more participation and generates a broader range of views, some of which may be refreshingly unique. It's easier to tone down and adapt a wild suggestion than to pump up a mediocre one.

Ask open-ended, unbiased questions that respect your workers' views and draw them out. For example:

"What would you do if . . .?"

"You're closest to the situation. What do you think about . . .?"

"Since you know this job better than I do, how would
you deal with . . . ?"

Attack the problem, not those who may have caused it. According to Charles Garfield, president of Performance Sciences Corporation, "Peak performers concentrate on solving problems rather than placing blame for them."

Word your questions carefully because people may say only what they think you want to hear. Information that's meant to agree with your thinking is of little value, so if you have ideas about the problem's cause or potential solutions, keep them to yourself for now.

Once you've asked, listen. Use steady eye contact and supportive nods to keep people talking, and be alert for "iceberg tips"—body language, facial expressions, gestures, and vague comments that hint that an employee might contribute more information or opinions if encouraged. For example, a human resources manager in one store of a large retailing chain made it a habit to sincerely ask employees, "How's everything going today?" One morning a salesperson replied, "Oh, all right, I guess." Sensing a problem, he asked, "Is there something I should know about?" Indeed there was. She proceeded to outline a storewide morale problem that rank-and-file employees were getting ready to take straight to top management. Fast action by the human resources manager resolved the matter within a week without top management's knowledge or involvement.

Give people time to mull over your request for information and develop some ideas. Putting them under a tight deadline inhibits open-minded thinking. Time permitting, it's better to say, "Let's get together in a few days and bounce this around. In the meantime, give it some thought. I'd like to have at least ____ suggestions we might check out." A little incubation time can often hatch a larger and more productive batch of recommendations about the problem's root cause or what may be done to solve it. Solving problems, however, is best done by following an orderly process. See Figure 6-1.

The Decision-Making Process
Step One: Define the Problem

The success of every later step in the process depends on clearly answering one key question: "What's *really* wrong?" If you're not

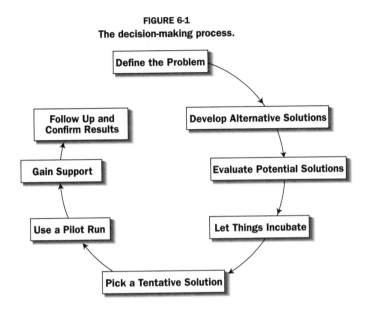

FIGURE 6-1
The decision-making process.

familiar with the area where the problem is, ask the people involved what they think is wrong. This is virtually always a good move because when you involve people in troubleshooting a problem, you also give them a vested interest in solving it. So be a democratic leader; practice participative management. This approach can help you avoid false starts, backtracking, wheel spinning, and serious losses later on. That's what happened with the ill-fated IBM PCjr. Its so-called Chicklet keyboard had a key shape and touch that felt odd to many users. That mistake probably wouldn't have happened if management had asked secretaries and word processing employees to use prototype models and had asked for their opinions.

When you're trying to define a problem, don't be fooled by symptoms. Symptoms give you clues about what's wrong, but they're not what you need to solve. For example, if the number of rejected parts skyrockets in one department, that's a symptom; it's not actually the problem. The problem is whatever is *causing* those rejects. It could be faulty materials, employee sabotage, improperly adjusted equipment, or a host of other possibilities. If you find a flat tire on your car tomorrow morning, the flat tire is merely a symptom. Pumping up the tire is a quick fix but not a genuine solution because the tire will only go flat again sooner or later. What caused the air to leak out is the real problem, and you (or a service station attendant) need to identify and fix it before your troubles will be over.

Step Two: Develop Alternative Solutions

Once you believe you've identified the true problem, generate as many solutions as possible. This step usually presents another good opportunity to involve employees by saying, "Now that we think we know what's wrong, what do we think we can do to fix it?"

If the nature of the problem and the time you have to solve it permit, a brainstorming session might be valuable. Call together everyone with a stake in solving the problem and ask each one to suggest any solution that comes to mind, no matter how bizarre or impractical it may seem. The ground rules of brainstorming demand a totally freewheeling meeting where nobody criticizes anyone else's comments and everyone feels free to suggest original solutions and build on or modify those proposed by other members of the group.

The major goal of a brainstorming session is to generate as many potential solutions as possible, no matter how unusual they might be. It's usually easier to modify a really wild idea into a workable solution than to try to pump life into a lukewarm suggestion that may produce mediocre results at best. Ingenuity is the key. If you organize a brainstorming session, prohibit group members from voicing "creativity killers" such as:

"Don't be ridiculous."

"It's too early (late) for that."

"We've never tried that before."

"The union will complain."

"It's worked just fine until now."

"We can't afford it."

"Higher management would never okay it."

"It won't work in our department."

"That's not our problem."

Some managers make a ground rule that anyone who makes a negative or critical comment during a brainstorming session must pay a dollar into the kitty. The money can be used to buy refreshments after the meeting.

Step Three: Evaluate Potential Solutions

The fun starts to fade away now because this step is a reality check. Here's where you screen the solutions you've produced against such limits as your budget; available people, time, and equipment; policies, procedures, and rules; and other factors beyond your control. Although this process of elimination weeds out actions that are clearly not doable, it will probably leave several possible solutions on the table to carry forward.

Step Four: Let Things Incubate

At this point, it's time for you to put your feet up on the desk and let the whole matter simmer on your mental back burner. Have you ever written a letter, put it away for a day or two, and reread it before you mailed it? If so, you can appreciate the value of incubation.

During incubation, your conscious and subconscious minds sort things out and view the problem and possible solutions from new angles. Don't be surprised, too, if a new solution or two comes to mind. Let a psychiatrist or psychologist worry about the subconscious mechanics of the process. They're not important. The point here is, good things may happen on your way to a decision if you let things simmer for a while. If nothing else, incubation prevents you from making a snap decision, which is frequently the same as tossing a coin.

Step Five: Pick a Tentative Solution

You can't incubate a decision forever. Sooner or later, you'll have to decide which one of several potential solutions seems to be the best. Your choice will be based on information that you and your employees uncovered during the third step (evaluation), as well as the insights, perspective, and modifications that may have surfaced while you let things incubate.

Notice, however, that this step mentions a *tentative* solution. That correctly implies that you should pilot-run the favored solution to a critical decision before you make a 100 percent commitment.

Step Six: Use a Pilot Run if Possible

Which decisions should you pilot-run? Generally speaking, any decision that could have a significant and negative impact on your career and reputation, the success of your employer and your department, and the careers and general welfare of your employees. A pilot run or pretest uncovers bugs in a major decision and helps you fine-tune it before you "go public" with it. The logic is simple: you're safer to risk a little by testing a decision on a limited basis than to bet the rent while flying blind.

Savvy managers pilot-run high-risk decisions whenever possible. For example, fast-food chains test new menu items extensively before going nationwide. Companies test new information-reporting and computer systems extensively before changing over from the old method. A new piece of production equipment may be installed and run parallel to the machine it'll replace until all the kinks have been worked out. New employees may have to work through a probationary period before their employment becomes final. Granted, some of these situations involve top management decisions and millions of dollars of potential profit or loss, but the benefits of a pilot run are identical at lower levels, too.

A department manager in a large textile plant believed that new lighting would improve employees' visibility and thus raise the quality of their products, but the cost of new fixtures made the decision too risky without a trial run. What happened? He installed new lights in 20 percent of his area, monitored product quality from those machines, and used the superior quality statistics to justify making the capital outlay.

The management of one manufacturing company once decided, without doing a pilot run, to attach meters to the computer keyboards in the word processing department and pay employees according to the number of keys they struck during the day. The program was discontinued after employees were seen eating lunch with one hand and randomly banging away on their keyboards with the other!

A pilot run's results may reveal that a decision should be modified in several ways. You may even discover, in extreme cases, that a decision that looked good on paper bombed in practice and should be abandoned altogether. Regardless of the situation, a pilot run both clarifies and minimizes the risks connected with making a key decision.

Step Seven: Gain Support

If employees help you define a problem and generate and evaluate possible solutions, you may enjoy a firm base of support already. Support is vital in most cases, however, because you're rarely the only person involved in putting your decisions to work. Some otherwise sound decisions may be doomed to failure if the people who have to ensure their success refuse to support them beyond the letter of their job descriptions.

Circumstances may suggest that you also get your boss's endorsement. This is especially true when your decision cuts across departmental boundaries or otherwise affects areas or employees who aren't under your control. For example, let's say one of your decisions requires several other departments to change the format or frequency of the periodic reports that they issue. Your peer managers in those departments would probably complain about the changes you want them to make in their routine, especially if the changes involve considerable work. Having convinced your boss that your decision is justified, you may have to ask her to convince the heads of the other departments that the changes are worthwhile and direct that they be made.

Step Eight: Follow Up and Confirm Results

Although a pilot run can raise your level of confidence, a successful pilot run doesn't guarantee a successful overall decision. After all, the field test may have been poorly designed, conducted at the wrong time, or done in the wrong place. So don't jump to conclusions just because a pilot run works out well. That's only presumptive proof of a sound decision.

A follow-up confirms that things are working out as well as the pilot run implied. Five arguments favor follow-up.

1. If your pilot run didn't duplicate actual working conditions, it may have produced misleading results. Follow-up will reveal this.

2. Conditions may have changed during the time between the pilot run and the decision's full-scale adoption.

3. Your decision may need some additional changes or fine-tuning that weren't apparent during the pilot run.

4. People who were affected by your decision after it was implemented may have suggestions for making it work better.

5. Follow-up may reveal areas in your department or other departments where your action could be applied with equal or better results than it produced to date.

Talk to people who are doing the hands-on implementation. Ask them such questions as:

- Are things generally working out the way we thought they would? If not, why?

- What has caused new or unexpected problems with implementing our decision? What suggestions do you have for dealing with them?

- In what ways has our decision worked out better than we thought? Why is this so?

- What changes should we make at this point to improve the results so far?

- If we try this approach again, what should we do differently? What should we leave alone?

- Do you see other places in our department or other departments where what we're doing would improve operations somehow?

Limiting Factors on Decisions

Several factors will limit your decision-making flexibility and discretion. The final decision must coordinate and acknowledge all of them.

- *Time.* When a decision needed to be made yesterday, lack of time can force you to decide before you've gathered all the important facts or explored possible solutions thoroughly. For example, the amount of time allocated to a particular space shuttle flight influences decisions about the type and duration of certain on-board experiments and how certain in-flight problems might be solved. The risk of making a bad decision increases considerably when you're working under the pressure of a close deadline.

■ *Policies.* Decisions must conform to existing policies. Those that don't will be rejected automatically. For example, policies may specify which vendors you're allowed to buy materials, supplies, and parts from, and you wouldn't be allowed to buy from a company that wasn't on the approved list no matter how good the deal seemed to be.

■ *Money.* Money is often the most restrictive and insurmountable influence on decisions. Sometimes you'll have to reject a preferred decision because you simply can't afford to do it.

■ *Your personal background and experience.* It's very difficult to set these factors aside and look at the situation objectively. We're all products of our past to some extent, and that colors how we view many situations in management. For example, if quality assurance rejects a batch of products, an engineer may suspect design problems; a purchasing manager may blame suppliers for shipping faulty materials; a human resources manager may think it's caused by low morale on the production line; and a production manager may blame the machine operators for not monitoring the equipment properly.

■ *Impact on other departments.* Many times you'll have to consider what impact your decision will have on related departments. You can't decide in a vacuum.

It's not unusual for decisions that are made in one area to set off a chain reaction. That's why coordination and communication are so important. For example, if the engineers who were responsible for designing a car's engine decided to increase the engine's displacement and horsepower, that would trigger the need for a bigger engine compartment, radiator, transmission, and brake system as well as stronger suspension. All of these things would have to be acknowledged, discussed, and agreed upon among all the departments that were responsible for designing and building each related part.

■ *Available personnel.* Your employees, like other resources, are limited both in numbers and in skill. You may not have all the employees you need to implement a particular decision successfully, and/or they may not have the necessary experience or skills to make it work.

Set Clear Limits on Authority

Employees who are afraid to act on their own to carry out your decisions may try to bounce the ball back onto your court. Don't let that happen.

Clarify how far each employee can go without getting your approval. Remind employees who come back to your desk like homing pigeons to "touch base" or "get your input" that you neither want nor expect to be involved in the nuts and bolts of making the decision work. You may have involved them in deciding *what* to do, but now that the decision work is done, give them the authority to decide *how* to do it. This approach develops more confident, competent, and promotable employees and frees you to learn and grow within the limits of your own job.

Group Decision Making

Group decision making has several features to recommend it and some drawbacks as well. The technique should certainly be included in your decision maker's tool kit.

Advantages of Group Decisions

Group decisions can be superior to individual decisions for several reasons.

■ Groups are typically more objective than one person. A group can explore a decision from more angles, produce a clearer and more accurate view of the problem, and generate more possible solutions than could one person alone. If a decision will benefit from exploring several points of view, or if it calls for more expertise or experience than you have, consider forming a group.

■ Group decision making is an excellent way to give your employees experience with the entire decision-making process. They go through all the phases, although they're not held individually responsible for the outcome. Group decision making requires them to think and act like managers and therefore enhances their growth and promotion potential.

■ Group decisions are often supported more enthusiastically because members were involved throughout the process. Giving people a vested interest in a decision makes it their decision, not just yours. That increases the likelihood that they'll try harder to make it work.

Drawbacks of Group Decisions

Despite their advantages, group decisions have limitations.

■ Group decisions often take more time than one-person decisions. A group without a deadline and sense of purpose may drag out the decision-making process until time becomes critical or the problem becomes worse than it would have been if the decision hadn't been delayed and discussed to death.

■ Group members may negotiate, distort, and compromise a solution almost beyond recognition. This accounts for the wisecrack, "A camel is a horse that's been designed by a group." Although negotiation and compromise are often necessary, it's important not to let a group rob exceptional ideas and suggestions of their originality, spice, and fire.

■ Groups may fall victim to groupthink and end up agreeing with one another against their better judgment. People who succumb to peer pressure, don't speak their minds, and "go with the flow" to preserve harmony or avoid conflicts or bad feelings often make decisions that aren't in the best interests of the organization, and the decisions may turn out to be what nobody really wanted.

■ Group decisions can lose their objectivity if one group member who outranks the rest intimidates the others into supporting his or her idea or if group members trade favors in *Godfather* fashion ("If you support my proposal, I'll support one of yours later on").

Value Diversity

Culturally diverse employees can help managers make better-informed decisions on a broad range of problems. Here are some suggestions to help you acknowledge and take advantage of a multicultural work group.

■ Appreciate the fact that a diverse work group expands and enhances your ability to view problems more objectively and generate a larger number of creative solutions.

■ Use your diverse work group to obtain a wider variety of input about how acceptable and effective proposed solutions might be when a problem involves blending or reconciling cultural differences.

■ Demonstrate by both words and actions that you value the contributions and views of each employee who works for you.

■ Educate yourself. Read, listen, and learn about the cultural perceptions, customs, and practices that influence each employee's behavior, values, lifestyle, hobbies, and interests.

■ When taking a team approach to implementing decisions, select team members who represent an accurate cultural and ethnic cross-section of the employees in your department so that everyone feels consulted and involved.

Delegate Authority

Delegation, which is the act of passing down some of your authority to people who work for you, is one of the most valuable and versatile tools of the management trade. Effective delegators:

- Are comfortable accepting the risks that go along with delegating authority.

- Delegate as much as possible.

- Understand and appreciate how delegation can improve the performance, skill development, and potential of both themselves and the employees to whom they've delegated.

- Take the time to describe delegated assignments clearly.

- Follow up and encourage feedback after delegating an assignment.

- Tolerate employees' honest mistakes when things don't work out as planned.

- Analyze the task to be delegated and the abilities of available employees carefully before choosing a delegate.

- Understand the skills and abilities of employees thoroughly enough to make reasonably sound choices from among the available delegates.

- Are willing to delegate to relatively inexperienced employees in order to nurture their growth, development, confidence, and skills.

- Make sure they're accessible when employees need more information or advice about how to tackle a delegated assignment.

Unfortunately, many managers avoid delegation, fear it, or use it ineffectively because they:

- Worry that employees will make mistakes.

- Dislike sharing credit for success with those who work for them.

- Believe they don't have time to teach employees how to do the delegated work.

- Don't trust the methods or techniques employees would use.

- Prefer to retain total control over their job by doing everything themselves.

You've probably had bosses in your career who didn't delegate, or did so reluctantly, for similar reasons. The trouble is, poor delegators are frequently ineffective managers because they deny themselves the major benefits of delegation, which include:

- Having more time to solve unique problems and work on nonroutine tasks.

- Developing confident, competent employees who think for themselves and require minimal supervision.

- Placing decision-making authority in the hands of people who are closest to the problems or opportunities in question.

- Enhancing their own chance for advancement by preparing one or more employees to take over the job when a promotion becomes available.

Relating Authority, Responsibility, and Accountability

It's important to have a clear picture of how these three elements of delegation relate to each other.

Authority is your right to make decisions and direct the work of others. Every manager's job has some inherent degree of authority. When you delegate, you hand some of this authority down to the people who report to you.

Responsibility is the obligation to carry out an assigned task to the best of one's ability. Responsibility isn't delegated by a manager to an employee. It arises when the employee accepts the task that the manager has assigned.

Accountability is being answerable to others for the consequences—either good or bad—of one's actions. Employees who accept delegated tasks and the authority to carry them out become accountable for the results and must sometimes justify or explain their actions to their bosses. At the same time, delegating managers are accountable for how they use the authority inherent in their jobs and for the performance of the employees to whom they have delegated part of that authority.

Accountability forms a vertical chain inside an organization. In a corporation, for example, lower-level operators and nonsupervisory workers are at the bottom, and the board of directors is at the top. Each level is accountable to the one above it, including the board of directors (who must account to the stockholders). Note that authority and responsibility move in opposite directions. Authority is delegated from higher managers to the employees beneath them, but responsibility for results flows upward. Accountability moves vertically, with one level of managers directly answerable to the next level for the consequences of their actions.

It's also important to realize that growth leads to progressively greater delegation. The more an organization expands, the busier top managers become—and the less time they have to make important decisions. There aren't enough hours in a day. In such cases delegation becomes a survival skill.

Choosing the Best Person for the Task

Delegation involves more than just picking a warm body. Following an orderly, thoughtful selection routine helps you choose employees whose skills are most compatible with the job or pick those who should benefit most from the experience.

Analyze the Task and Candidates

Many supervisors underestimate the importance of a little preliminary analysis, but it's central to delegating work effectively. Consider the following four factors:

1. *How close is the deadline?* Rush jobs require time-oriented employees who can be counted on to come through under pressure. Consider available employees in light of their self-management ability and sense of responsibility both to themselves and to you. The tighter the deadline, the more you'll need to choose a conscientious person who will do the right thing and do it on time.

2. *How much coordination is needed?* Delegate assignments that demand lots of coordination or cooperation among colleagues or departments to consensus builders. Jobs that call for little interaction with other departments, however, might safely be delegated to your more headstrong, less diplomatic employees.

3. *How will the job help the person to grow?* Here's an excellent chance to help satisfy employees' training and development needs that came to light through performance evaluations. Check your files if necessary to identify people who would benefit most from this particular assignment. Consider, for example, the degree of challenge involved in the task; how much initiative, judgment, or discretion it calls for; and how well it will help the candidate develop written or spoken communication skills.

4. *How much innovation is involved?* Highly innovative assignments call for dreamers more than doers—people who, like the bird that built a nest with a hole in the bottom, thrive on creativity but dislike responsibility. On the other hand, tasks that involve a standard routine or plain old "grunt work" are best given to detail-minded systems builders who enjoy doing work that's been laid out for them.

In addition to the above factors, take time to weigh such influences as enthusiasm, ambition, and desire. Employees who get excited about learning new skills and mastering new techniques may do a better job than their more apathetic coworkers. Likewise, consider each candidate's ambition to grow, meet challenges, and acquire new experience. Finally, ask yourself which persons really seem to *want* the assignment and perhaps have told you so. Other things being equal, enthusiasm, ambition, and desire deserve to be acknowledged and rewarded.

What if Several People Are Qualified?

This is a welcome dilemma, but one that must be handled fairly in order to preserve high morale. One solution is to let the employees themselves decide who will get the job. This tactic, while admittedly frustrating, gives them experience with consensus building, compromise, and group dynamics. Make sure to clarify, however, that you've left the decision up to them for those reasons, and not because you're reluctant to make it yourself or exercise leadership.

An obvious alternative is to pick the person yourself, and if you do, make sure to promise those who were passed over that they'll get the next assignment that comes up. Finally, you might let several equally qualified candidates tackle the project as a team instead of assigning it to one person alone.

If there's no clear standout after you've analyzed the task and candidates, consider giving the job to the person (or perhaps a team of coworkers) who seems to need the experience most and/or possesses most of the skills that the job demands. Relative motivation may be an arbitrating factor here, too.

Explain Your Decision

Once you've made your decision, explain its rationale to the runners-up. This action is important because it minimizes claims of favoritism or discrimination. Be sure that everyone understands the criteria you used to make your selection and the reasons why you chose whom you did.

Discussing the Assignment

When you call in the person to discuss the assignment, highlight aspects of the project that may be especially challenging, but express your faith in the employee's ability to meet these challenges and grow with the experience. Each of us grows by being asked to stretch beyond our present limits; you compliment employees when you expect more from them than they may think they're capable of.

Last but not least, don't give the impression that the job's a sink-or-swim proposition. Be prepared to coach and be more accessible to marginally qualified persons, while taking care not to let them shift decisions onto your shoulders or use your availability as a crutch.

Defend Against Reverse Delegation

It's not unusual for employees to try to toss delegated work back into their manager's lap. Sometimes this happens because they're inadequately trained, they're afraid of making mistakes, they want to spread the blame if things go wrong, or they're reluctant to trust their own judgment.

Supervisors can employ several tactics to insulate themselves against reverse delegation and keep the authority where it's meant to be.

■ Verify, at least to yourself, that the person is in fact qualified to handle the task and express your confidence that she can do it successfully. Tactfully point out that the assignment is now part of the employee's responsibilities and will be included in the next performance evaluation.

■ Make sure there's a meeting of the minds. This might be done with a simple statement such as, "I want to make it clear that you'll be responsible for this from now on. Do you have any questions about that?" Doing so confirms that you intend to hold the employee accountable for results.

■ Develop standard responses that you can use whenever somebody tries to bounce an assignment back on you. Use these remarks consistently. For example:

> "I'm sure you can do this if you stick with it. Give it another try."

> "You need to master this skill as part of your development plan. I want you to have the experience."

"I gave you the assignment because I trust your judgment. I want the ball to stay in your court."

"I've become too busy to get involved with this job now. We'll have to go with your decision."

What Should You Do if Delegation Doesn't Work?

Delegation is an inexact science. If you see the employee falling short of standards, making mistakes, or acting frustrated with the task, it's easy to overreact by assuming the task yourself or giving it to someone else. Both actions may be wrong. Taking over the job denies employees the chance to straighten things out and redeem themselves. Transferring the job to a coworker makes the first employee lose face as well as an opportunity for growth.

When a delegated assignment doesn't meet your expectations, the best course is often to (1) review how you made the assignment, (2) resist the urge to recall the entire task, and (3) work with the confused employee until he learns to do the job right.

Review How You Made the Assignment

When you notice continuing signs of trouble, take a few minutes to mentally review how you delegated the job in the first place. More specifically, did you:

- Set clear performance standards?

- Explain the "how-to's" of the job thoroughly?

- Actively solicit the person's questions?

- Give the employee a model or example to measure performance against?

- Follow up after the task was assigned?

Although this exercise helps you troubleshoot your delegation technique (and perhaps correct some flaws), you'll have to go further to resolve your immediate problem.

Resist the Urge to Recall the Entire Task

Your first impulse might be to recall the job entirely and either do it yourself or assign it to someone else. The suggestion is: Don't. Over-reacting by taking back a task immediately can devastate a person's ego and cause smoldering resentment because you deny your employee a chance to fix the problem and set things right. No one likes to lose face and be branded a failure in front of coworkers. Savvy supervisors, like seasoned football coaches, don't bench rookie players because of one miscue.

Beyond your employee's feelings, however, you should think about what you'd be doing to yourself. Rescinding authority at the first sign of trouble makes you look impulsive and indecisive. In addition, your approach to the problem sets a precedent as far as other employees are concerned. They'll see your response as a model for how they might be treated under the same circumstances, and they'll react in one of two ways. Snatching back new tasks at the first sign of trouble will prompt some employees to sidestep your efforts to delegate work. They won't want to be treated as incompetents if they, too, have trouble doing a new job correctly. Others may be prone to do a careless job, knowing that you'll shift the burden back onto your own shoulders. As one employee put it, "Why should I worry about screwing up? The first time something goes wrong, my boss will jump in with both feet and do it himself!"

Work With the Confused Employee

Four steps can keep you from shooting from the hip or shooting yourself in the foot when delegation bogs down.

1. *Talk before you act.* Talk to the employee privately, review performance standards, and explain why the work hasn't been acceptable. Be specific; avoid vague remarks like, "Things aren't working out" or "I think I'd better reconsider what I gave you to do last week." People are typically hungry for details when their pride and performance are on the line. They won't be satisfied with generalities. Would you?

This conference also gives you an opportunity to establish a sense of obligation and joint commitment. After all, both of you have a stake in the outcome and a shared interest in seeing that the job in question is done correctly.

Ask the employee to propose actions that would resolve the problem, and tactfully suggest that more training, preparation, or authority might be in order. If the person feels ill-equipped to do the task because of one of those factors, you've made it easier to say so. Without some encouragement, people are embarrassed to admit that they're treading water.

This is also an ideal time to review the "how-to's" of the job once again. Recap your original instructions carefully (avoid remarks like "This is self-explanatory"), and welcome the employee's questions by asking open-ended questions of your own that presume you haven't explained everything clearly. For example:

> "What else should we go over?"
>
> "Which part of the job do we need to talk about some more?"
>
> "What activities do you feel unclear about?"

If the delegated job has a tangible result that can be demonstrated (such as a properly formatted report or a specific production routine), set up an example that the employee can use as a model. This may be all that's necessary to eliminate confusion and put things back on an even keel.

If the job consists of a central task and several satellite tasks, your employee's comments during this meeting might suggest that you take back some of the lesser ones temporarily. Doing so would give the person more time to master the core task without getting lost in details. When saddled with a major responsibility and a host of secondary tasks, some people panic before they get their arms around it all. "I simply couldn't juggle all the new details at once," one frustrated person confessed. "I felt like I was trying to nail Jell-O to a tree."

2. *Get closure on this conference.* The above conference should close with a clear understanding of which parts of the job, if any, you'll take back and which ones will be left with your employee. In addition, make sure the two of you agree on the standards that must be met, and establish a timetable for following up on progress. This timetable is especially important because it keeps lines of communication open, provides a built-in excuse for making future contact, and assures the person that she isn't being left to sink or swim.

The conference and its resulting closure speak well for you as a boss. You come across as a cool-headed coach and counselor instead of an impulsive dictator or a whip-cracking galleymaster. Your worker knows what is wrong and why, and has an action list and perhaps a model to follow to bring the work up to standard by a specific deadline.

3. *Back up your words with action.* Monitor your employee's performance regularly, realizing that she may be anxious or defensive because of the circumstances. Show concern without over-supervising, and follow up with open-ended requests or questions such as, "Tell me how everything is going" and "Which problems should we discuss?" Make an effort to praise improvement whenever praise is justified. Praise alleviates anxiety and confirms that the person is making progress.

4. *Delegate additional parts of the job as performance improves.* Any satellite duties that you took back in step 1 can be redelegated as performance improves and the person gains confidence. Consider relaying these tasks piecemeal, however, so your employee can integrate them into the existing routine gradually. Passing them down all at once may trigger another round of confusion and frustration.

When you add a new segment of the job, make certain to explain its importance and emphasize how it relates to the work previously assigned. This technique helps the employee see the task both as a whole and as the sum of its parts—to see the forest as well as the trees.

Skill Comes With Practice

Experienced supervisors realize that delegation is an acquired skill. Relaying work to employees successfully takes practice and the willingness to work with people who may have trouble handling an entire job all at once. Managers who are willing to help their employees over some early rough spots build a working bond that ensures that they, their employees, and the entire organization grow beyond yesterday's skills to master the challenges of tomorrow.

Hiring and Orienting New People

Managers who hire and orient qualified new employees enhance the success of their departments and organization many times over. These related activities are instrumental in maximizing productivity and morale and minimizing turnover. This chapter suggests some practical techniques that will sharpen your ability to recruit and hire proficient people and help them get their feet on the ground once they're on the payroll.

Recruiting

Although the human resources department usually plays an active role in locating potential employees, managers sometimes find that recruiting applicants falls within their job responsibilities as well. In any event, it's essential to have reliable sources of qualified applicants before you can actively begin the hiring process.

Where can you go for these qualified applicants? See Figure 8-1.

FIGURE 8-1.
Sources of qualified applicants.

Present Employees	Applications on File	Employee Recommendations	Advertising	Private Employment Agencies	State Employment Agencies	Misc.

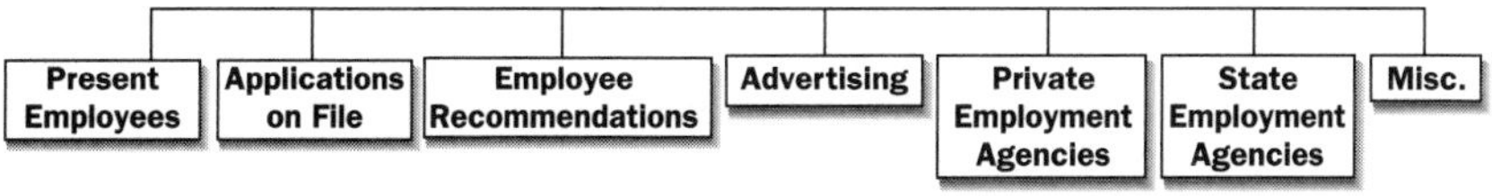

■ *Present Employees (Recruiting from within).* Your existing workforce is the least expensive and most convenient source of candidates for job openings. Qualified employees who are promoted into vacant positions are proof that higher management genuinely means to provide growth opportunities for everyone. The experience of seeing deserving peers rewarded with advancement boosts employees' morale across the board. Filling vacant jobs with existing employees also saves the time and cost of orienting outside people to the way your company operates. At the very least, your present employees should already understand major policies, procedures, and general operations and may only have to be prepared for the duties of the new position they've been moved into.

■ *Applications on file.* Unsolicited walk-in applications are an inexpensive source of potential employees. Applications should be cross-referenced among all the positions that candidates seem qualified for.

■ *Employee recommendations.* Present employees may be asked to recommend friends and relatives (nepotism policy permitting) for vacant positions. Because people are often reluctant to stake their reputations on someone else's performance, applicants whom present employees recommend frequently prove to be top-quality workers.

In times of high employment, employers commonly offer a reward or "bounty" to employees who recommend applicants for highly skilled or hard-to-fill positions. Rewards have ranged anywhere from a $25,000 sports car (for people who were ultimately hired to fill engineering and software design positions) to cash awards and Hawaiian vacations.

■ *Advertising.* Ads in trade and professional magazines may be used to attract applicants for exotic technical jobs and higher-level positions in such areas as engineering, purchasing, finance, and human resources management. When recruiting for lower-level positions, companies such as McDonald's have even used such simple and offbeat approaches as printing mini-applications on their placemats. Walt Disney World has posted large "Disney Works for Me" help-wanted billboard ads throughout central Florida, and BellSouth has inserted ads describing job opportunities in its telephone directories, where they're likely to be seen.

■ *Private employment agencies.* These companies can save you a great deal of time and paperwork by screening applicants according to your specifications and forwarding the best-qualified ones to you. Some agencies specialize in placing certain types of people such as engineers.

■ *State employment agencies.* State employment agencies are productive sources of nonmanagerial applicants, as well as semiskilled and unskilled workers. When unemployment is high, they can provide management-level and skilled applicants as well. As a rule, however, highly specialized applicants and those who are looking for positions in middle management or above are usually recruited through private employment agencies and other sources.

■ *Miscellaneous sources.* These might include, for example, trade and technical schools and community colleges with so-called tech prep programs that train students for narrowly defined jobs in such areas as graphic design technology, electronics engineering technology, dental hygiene, diagnostic medical sonography, and medical transcription; job fairs held by a consortium of local educational institutions; neighborhood and community groups; local chapters of professional societies; and social service agencies.

Hiring

Once you've established a steady supply of quality applicants from a combination of the above sources, you'll need to hire the best qualified ones when job vacancies occur.

Compare the Job Specification With the Application

The human resources department usually prepares a specification for each job. A job specification summarizes the minimum training, experience, special skills, education, and other essential qualities an applicant must have in order to do the job satisfactorily. For example, an administrative assistant's job specification might read as follows:

Knowledge, Skills, and Abilities

■ Ability to use an IBM-compatible personal computer

■ Keyboarding speed of 60 correct words per minute

- Capable of conducting information searches via the Internet and the World Wide Web

- Thorough understanding of all major functions of Microsoft Word and Microsoft Excel computer programs

- Demonstrated competence in spelling, punctuation, grammar usage, and composition

- Demonstrated ability to handle multiple priorities, organize work, and function independently

- Sound interpersonal communication skills

Experience

- A minimum of four years' secretarial experience in positions of increasing responsibility or three years secretarial experience and an Associate in Science degree in Office Systems Technology from an accredited institution

Working Conditions

- Sedentary work that requires frequent contact with the public in person, by telephone, and by e-mail

Review the job specification's requirements and compare them with the information applicants provided on the application blank. Those who are clearly unqualified may be eliminated at this point; those who have "the right stuff" (at least on paper) may be called in for a personal interview.

Interviewing Suggestions

Before you interview the most promising applicants, review the position's job description.

- Make certain that you understand the duties and responsibilities of the job you're hiring for.

- Decide which interview format (discussed later in this chapter) is appropriate for the circumstances.

- Develop specific questions that will help you assess the applicant's qualifications in light of information provided on the application blank.

The job description for the administrative assistant's position mentioned above might list the following duties that you would want to discuss during the interview:

- May be assigned to hire, evaluate, guide, and review the work of other clerical staff assigned to the division.

- Provides day-to-day secretarial support and coordination of the division's clerical activities.

- Assembles data and prepares detailed, confidential reports on a routine and as-needed basis.

- Composes and prepares correspondence for the division manager's signature.

- Composes and is responsible for routine internal communications related to the division's administrative functions.

- Thoroughly understands relevant policies and procedures and the division's operations and activities.

- Provides information and makes minor administrative decisions in the division manager's absence.

- Independently locates information and resolves issues and problems without referring them to a superior.

- Acts as a liaison between the division manager and other employees, departments, and divisions.

- Receives and screens incoming calls and places outgoing calls for the division manager.

- Establishes and maintains division filing systems for both confidential and nonconfidential information.

- Maintains an appointment calendar and uses discretion in scheduling appointments and meetings for the division manager.

■ Coordinates meeting arrangements, reserves meeting rooms, and prepares meeting materials as directed.

■ Maintains a supply of forms and clerical materials for the assigned area. Designs or recommends forms needed to accomplish the division's objectives.

Productive interviews happen through conscious effort. When it's time to conduct interviews with applicants, enhance the value of your interviewing time by following these nine general guidelines.

1. Make a list of the specific topics you want to discuss or areas that need to be clarified based on information on the person's application blank and the job specification and description.

2. Pick a comfortable location that's free from phone calls, drop-in visitors, and other interruptions.

3. Put the applicant at ease with some "small talk." Be cordial, informal, and conversational. Don't sound like an interrogator.

4. Answer the applicant's questions about the job and your organization early in the interview.

5. Be objective. Guard against making positive or negative judgments based on an applicant's personality, appearance, or personal information. *Concentrate on assessing the applicant's qualifications for the job.*

6. Listen more than you talk. Nondirective questions (those that can't be answered yes or no) encourage applicants to express their honest feelings and opinions.

7. Listen critically. Make a mental note of interview topics that produced evasive, volatile, enthusiastic, inconsistent, emotional, or otherwise memorable responses.

8. Conclude the interview by thanking applicants for their time and telling them how long it will be before you'll make a decision. Don't leave them hanging in suspense. Your courtesy may pay off in goodwill and their willingness to reapply later if additional vacancies occur.

9. Record your impressions, the applicant's answers to key questions, and information about the topics you wanted to cover in your preinterview notes as soon as you've concluded the interview.

Interview Formats

You can use a directive, nondirective, or combination interview. The choice depends on your experience, the amount of time you have for interviewing, and the nature of the job you have to fill.

A *directive interview* follows a standardized list of questions. Although this format tends to be somewhat rigid, it places you in firm control of the conversation and ensures that you'll cover all the major topics in a minimum length of time. Directive interviews are sometimes favored by inexperienced interviewers, but its checklist approach can make you sound like a hard-boiled inquisitor. What's more, applicants will have few chances to volunteer additional information that might influence your hiring decision.

A *nondirective interview* is extremely flexible; it uses open-ended questions instead of a cut-and-dried format. Approach it with a general idea of the information you want from the applicant, and phrase your questions to create rapport, reveal attitudes, and elicit opinions and responses that may disclose more information about an applicant's qualifications than directive interviews tend to do.

Conducting a nondirective interview takes experience, however. For one thing, you must be able to steer the conversation back on course when applicants ramble off on a tangent or get hung up on a particular subject. You'll also have to make sure that you cover all the topics that you wanted to discuss when you compared the person's application against the job specification.

A *combination interview* blends both directive and nondirective techniques. Many managers use it for that reason. For example, you can start with a directive format to cover basic information on the application:

> "What specific types of heavy equipment are you qual-
> ified to operate?"

> "Why were you laid off by XYZ Inc.?"

> "Your application says you were unemployed from _____
> to _____. Tell me what you did during that time."

"Which desktop PC programs can you run?"

"I see you're working toward your G.E.D. When will you be finished?"

You can switch from a directive to a nondirective format to discuss and evaluate career goals, communication skills, persuasiveness, dependability, temperament, ambition, self-motivation, and human relations skills. Examples of general-purpose nondirective questions are as follows:

"Why do you want to work for our company?"

"What job(s) are you most interested in?"

"What did you enjoy about your most recent job?"

"What did you like least about your most recent job?"

"Tell me about the toughest deadline you've ever met." What was the situation? Who was involved? What happened?"

"Tell me about the last time a supervisor asked you to do something and you didn't get it done on time. Describe the situation. What did you do about it? What happened?"

"Tell me about a new work system or procedure that you had trouble learning. What was it? Why was it difficult for you to learn? How did you finally master it?"

"Tell me about the last time you had to do something that wasn't covered by normal procedures. How did the situation come up? What did you do? What happened? What do you usually do in situations like that?"

"Tell me about one of your coworkers who was hard to get along with. Describe the situation that upset you the most. How did you react? How did it affect the work?"

"Tell me about a time when you did something that was above and beyond your regular job responsibilities. What kind of situation was it? What did you do that was so exceptional?"

"What feedback, if any, did you get from your boss or coworkers?"

"Give me an example of a mistake that you've learned from. What was it? What did you learn? How did you handle that situation afterward?"

"If I talked to the people who worked with you on a project you were responsible for, what would they tell me about how you handled the job?"

"Describe the best boss you've ever had and why."

"Describe the worst boss you've ever had and why."

"Tell me about a job that required you to work as a member of a team. What did you like most about the experience? What did you like least?"

"Describe your greatest strengths and weaknesses."

"Describe yourself the way you think your former boss would describe you."

"How would you describe your ideal job?"

"If you finished an assignment early, how would you use the leftover time?"

"How would you react if you asked somebody in another department for information and he or she told you to get lost?"

"What do you see yourself doing _____ years from now?"

"How do you motivate yourself to do an unpleasant job?"

"What kind of people do you like to work with?"

Legal Concerns

Federal and state employment laws try to ensure that everyone has equal access and opportunity to jobs and promotions. They're specifically meant to protect racial and religious minorities, women, the handicapped, and people between the ages of forty and seventy.

While claims of hiring discrimination are extremely hard to prove, no one wants to get hauled into court. Unfortunately, there's no neat list of illegal questions. Even if you don't mean to discriminate, the implications of some questions that managers could ask during an employment interview may prompt a court to declare them (and your organization) discriminatory. For example, asking if an applicant can work on weekends may seem innocent, but courts may rule it discriminatory if your only reason is based on religious beliefs.

Interview questions must be strictly job-related. Avoid questioning applicants about such areas as:

- Race, color, ethnic background, or family history

- Language usually spoken at home

- Membership in ethnic clubs or organizations

- Marital status

- Birth control, family planning, children's ages, or child-care arrangements

- Spouse's occupation

- Sexual orientation or preferences

- Church attended or religious beliefs and practices

- Nature or extent of disabilities

- Medical history

- Age or birth date

- Arrest records

- Wage attachments or garnishment

Also, you cannot ask questions that are asked of one sex only. For example, you cannot ask only female applicants if they can type.

If all this information frustrates you, join the club. Perhaps the simplest guideline of all is to focus on interview questions and selection criteria that relate to the applicant's qualifications for and ability to perform the job you have to fill. If you do so, you'll be headed in the right direction.

Orientation: Where Do We Go From Here?

Have you ever been tossed into a job and left to sink or swim? If so, you know how important thorough orientation can be. It was mentioned earlier that sound hiring decisions, followed by thorough orientation, minimize turnover and boost productivity and morale. In addition, savvy managers cash in on orientation's opportunity to hit new employees with all the positive aspects about the job, department, and organization before their enthusiasm is dulled by the cynical views of coworkers whose enthusiasm may have diminished.

Some of the more common information that should be covered during orientation includes:

- Mission statement

- Code of ethics

- Commitment to equal employment opportunities

- Policies, procedures, and rules governing the custody and safe-keeping of confidential information and materials such as customer databases, computer passwords, proprietary software and operating systems, key cards, and access to high-security areas

- Compensation and fringe benefits

- Employee communications channels (e-mail, voice mail, newsletters, bulletin boards, and other media)

Larger organizations have highly detailed orientation procedures that typically include a checklist of orientation topics managers are required to cover during the first several days and weeks. If you're working for a smaller and less formal company, however, your orientation responsibilities may be much less clear. If that's the case, here's a five-step process to help your new hires get up to speed ASAP and feel comfortable in their jobs and with their colleagues.

1. Have the new employee fill out all payroll and personnel forms if the personnel department hasn't already done so. Explain options about insurance coverage, income tax withholding, the 401-K plan, and other relevant subjects.

2. Review each duty and responsibility listed on the employee's job description. Emphasize that you may ask the person to do certain work that isn't specifically mentioned (unless such requests are prohibited by a union contract or other agreement). It's often important to clarify this so employees understand management's need for reasonable flexibility in making work assignments. If you're a team-based organization, emphasize the job's team-oriented duties and responsibilities.

3. Give the employee a copy of the employee handbook and related literature that cover such topics as company history, health and life insurance programs, retirement benefits, credit union, tuition reimbursement, employee assistance program, employee suggestion program, total quality management, and child-care assistance.

Explain all relevant policies, procedures, and rules. These may include, but certainly won't be limited to, appropriate workplace behavior, acceptable attire, affirmative action, timekeeping, promotions, pay raises, discipline, performance evaluation, vacations, holidays, sick leave, funeral leave, maternity leave, lateness and absenteeism, layoffs and recalls, break periods, lunchtime, overtime pay, and the correct use of safety equipment. Answer all the new worker's questions; if in doubt, contact the personnel department.

4. Show how the new person's job relates to the other jobs in your department, how it affects the work of colleagues in related departments, and how your department integrates with other departments and with the entire facility. An organization chart can be very useful here; it makes this information clear and easy to understand and gives the new employee a mental model of how everything's supposed to fit.

Supervisors in team-based organizations should consider flow-charting responsibilities both within and among work teams. A flow-chart illustrates and dramatizes key relationships among team members and their counterparts on the teams they interact with. You might also have new hires shadow each team member for a certain length of time, then meet with all of them as a group to discuss their relative roles, talk about the new employee's responsibilities, and resolve any questions or misunderstandings.

5. Take the newcomer on a walking tour of your department and surrounding areas. Point out the location of break rooms, restrooms, lockers, mail facilities, and copy machines. Introduce the person to everyone in your department and to coworkers in other departments that she will have to work with frequently. As you do, share some personal information that may create rapport among them and help to break the ice ("Helen's is a big fan of the Kansas City Chiefs"; "Joe's restoring a '77 Pontiac Grand Prix"; "Tim's President of the Lions Club"; "Stacey just got back from a vacation in Las Vegas").

Make certain the new employee feels free to ask questions. Keep yourself accessible; assume the person will feel uncertain, confused, and somewhat frustrated for the next few days. Although orientation may be mostly your responsibility, you may want to match up the new hire with an experienced employee who knows the ropes. This "buddy system" may be a good idea, since new people are often more comfortable discussing questions or admitting ignorance to peers than to a supervisor. If you do use a buddy system, make sure the senior employee is committed to being a conscientious mentor and takes the responsibility seriously (see Chapter 7's discussion of delegation).

Motivate Your People

M otivated employees invest more of themselves in their jobs than they're required to do. They reach beyond the boundaries of their job descriptions and push the limits of their abilities, not because they *have* to but because they *want* to. They go the extra mile to make sure that the people they serve, whether internal colleagues or external customers, are fully satisfied.

Motivated people not only do things right, they also do the right thing, and do it willingly. Managers who are effective motivators:

- Attempt to be sound role models for employees to pattern themselves after.

- Refuse to bend or break policies, procedures, and rules to suit their own convenience.

- Set challenging goals for themselves and expect and encourage their employees to do likewise.

- Go to great lengths to ensure that their employees receive appropriate praise and recognition for their accomplishments.

- Would never take credit for their employees' ideas and achievements.

- Believe that employees are looking for more from their work than material rewards such as pay and fringe benefits.

- Assign the type of work to employees that will help them improve and expand their skills, exercise their own initiative, gain confidence in their own abilities, and qualify for advancement.

- Use delegation as a motivational tool whenever appropriate.

- Give employees the opportunity to participate in decisions that will affect their jobs or working environment whenever possible.

You learned about effective hiring practices in the preceding chapter for a very good reason. Sound hiring makes motivating employees infinitely easier. Think about your own experience. Have you ever had a job you simply didn't like, even though you were qualified to do it? If so, how much success did your boss have in motivating *you* to do more than absolutely necessary? The odds are, very little. But if you start by selecting "motivatable" applicants who enjoy the basic nature of the work they've been hired to do, your chances of motivating them to turn in above-average performance increase considerably. The feelings of employees who may be qualified but "unmotivatable" are often expressed on the bumper sticker that says, "I love my job. It's the work I hate."

Be a Positive Role Model

Effective motivation begins with *you* because the enthusiasm and motivation you display toward your job is contagious. Employees tend to adopt their boss's traits, values, standards, and work habits. Managers who step into the breach and move forward on their own initiative are positive role models. Instead of cajoling, threatening, or cheerleading, they take command, lead by example, and demand as much from themselves as they do from their staff. Their motto might be, "Do as I say *and* as I do."

How can you be a positive role model? Let's start with the basics. Arrive at work on time; be punctual with appointments; return calls promptly; respect and follow policies, procedures, and rules; set challenging goals for yourself; support strict quality standards; and put in longer hours and greater effort when necessary to honor your commitments to internal and external customers.

Positive role models are also loyal to the team. You can demonstrate your loyalty by demanding recognition for your group's achievements and bringing those achievements to higher management's attention. Make sure to give your employees their fair share of any praise that comes your way. In management, as in sports, it takes a team effort to bring home the trophy.

Motivational Theorists Whose Theories Work in Practice

Textbooks discuss many motivational theorists, but here you'll get acquainted with three whose viewpoints are especially relevant to rookie managers.

Douglas McGregor

A professor of industrial management, Douglas McGregor placed managers into one of two categories—Theory X or Theory Y—according to the managers' basic assumptions about their employees. The assumptions a manager makes affects the way he or she deals with subordinates—and hence the way they're likely to respond.

According to McGregor, a Theory X manager is one who believes that people work mainly for money, are lazy and irresponsible, won't think for themselves, cannot be trusted, require close supervision, and must be pressured or threatened before they'll perform up to par. Such negative "I'm paid to think and you're paid to work" assumptions typically give rise to negative employee performance. Managers who expect the worst from their employees give them no incentive to do more than they absolutely have to.

A Theory Y manager, on the other hand, believes that people want more from their jobs than a paycheck and are basically ambitious and trustworthy. They enjoy challenge, welcome opportunities to show their ingenuity, and need minimal supervision once they understand and have mastered the basic skills they need to do their jobs. In other words, Theory Y managers tend to follow a democratic or laissez-faire leadership style. Their Theory X colleagues are classic autocrats. See Figure 9-1.

FIGURE 9-1
Douglas McGregor's Theory X and Theory Y managers.

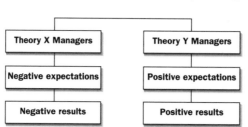

What level of performance are these two types of managers likely to get from their people? Usually the level that they seem to expect. Since Theory X bosses expect the worst, why should their employees try to do better than average? There's little reason to exceed the norm if your boss has low expectations and a negative opinion of you. Theory Y bosses, by contrast, expect people to live up to their standards and may even ask employees to do more than the employees themselves believe they're capable of. The results can be highly rewarding, however. If you select the most qualified people, and let them know you expect their best performance, they'll often respond by doing their best not to disappoint you.

It's important to realize, however, that not every person or situation will respond positively to positive Theory Y expectations. For example, it's a workplace reality that some people simply don't like the jobs they're qualified to do or have fallen out of love with them through no fault of their own. In this case, no amount of Theory Y expectations from a boss can make them more self-challenging or willing to go the extra mile. Other low-performing employees may be well matched with their work but require more direction and supervision because they lack self-confidence or haven't fully mastered their responsibilities yet.

Some management situations won't respond well to a Theory Y approach either. For example, emergencies may require a Theory X response because time is short and someone has to step in, take command, and get things moving forward immediately. In addition, emotionally charged decisions that contain few or no positive elements (such as downsizing) may have to be made in a unilateral Theory X fashion.

Frederick Herzberg

Herzberg contended that motivation is affected by two sets of job-related factors. Maintenance factors are the basic things that workers believe they're entitled to, such as adequate pay, satisfactory working conditions, and competitive fringe benefits. People who don't receive these basics will be dissatisfied and may even resign. If they do receive them, however, they aren't motivated. Who was ever motivated by fair treatment?

What does motivate people, according to Herzberg, is a chance to grow within their present job and to be promoted. Praise for work well done and a basic liking for the work itself are additional motivational factors.

Herzberg's message to managers is to give employees the basic or maintenance factors that you know they expect (and will be dissatisfied without), then load in as many motivational factors as possible to provide satisfaction and foster motivation. See Figure 9-2.

FIGURE 9-2
Frederick Herzberg's maintenance factors and motivational factors.

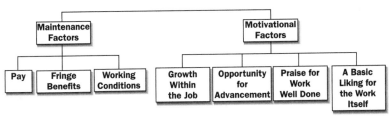

Abraham Maslow

Maslow's theory of motivation is much broader than either McGregor's or Herzberg's theories. (See Figure 9-3.)

FIGURE 9-3
Maslow's hierarchy of needs.

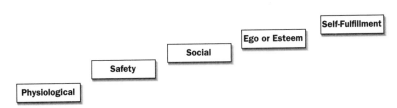

■ Employees' needs are arranged in order of importance from the most basic needs (water, food, and shelter) to the most complex (esteem and self-fulfillment).

■ Satisfied needs don't motivate people, simply because they can be met whenever they arise. It's the *un*satisfied needs that drive people to expend greater effort, and people usually recognize and attempt to fulfill them in the order shown in Figure 9-3. For example, someone who has just been promoted isn't likely to feel the need for esteem.

■ People will attempt to satisfy each need level before recognizing and being moved to satisfy the need at the next higher level.

■ If a need can't be satisfied each time it arises, it will become a priority once again. For example, someone who has a satisfying social life but is suddenly laid off will become obsessed with finding another job to satisfy physiological needs, which will suddenly take precedence over all others.

Physiological needs are the most basic of all, such as the need for food, drink, and shelter. If they're not satisfied, people won't even recognize, let alone attempt to fulfill, the needs beyond that level. Logically enough, these needs are commonly met by an adequate paycheck, although such workplace comforts as water fountains, air conditioning, ergonomically designed workstations, and protection from unpleasant odors and noises as well as fringe benefits such as health insurance, a 401-K investment program, paid vacations, and employee discounts are also offered.

After physiological needs are satisfied (or can be satisfied whenever they arise), people will recognize the existence of *safety needs*. These can be both physical safety (such as a nonhazardous working environment) and psychological safety (such as the job security provided by a union contract, seniority, a tenured faculty position at a college or university, or possessing an especially unique or critical skill that might tend to protect an employee from being laid off).

Employees who have generally covered the first two need levels on Maslow's hierarchy become aware of and attempt to satisfy the third one in line—*social needs*. The need to be accepted and included as part of a group can be met by membership on a formal work team and being part of an informal peer group that meets for lunch and gets together socially after working hours. In addition, social needs are often met through membership in such nonwork groups as fraternal organizations, college alumni and booster clubs, professional societies, service clubs, and, of course, relationships with friends and family members.

The next higher need level, that for *esteem* or *ego satisfaction*, relates to one's desire for a sense of value, self-worth, identity, and respect. This need level can be satisfied by a host of experiences, including praise and recognition from members of higher management, promotion to a job with greater status and responsibility, a pat on the back by one's immediate boss, an achievement award from a professional organization, or accomplishments that have nothing at all to do with work *per se*, such as excelling at a satisfying hobby such as restoring classic cars, moonlighting as a published novelist, or becoming a nationally recognized authority on Siamese cats.

The highest need level of all, *self-fulfillment*, is one that's rarely attained. This is the need to feel that you're getting all you can out of your life's experience.

Maslow estimated that only about 10 percent of people are truly self-fulfilled at any given time. Moreover, people who do feel genuinely self-fulfilled for the moment discover that the feeling is only temporary. The novelty of the experiences that presently make them self-fulfilled wears off as time goes by, and they begin searching for other experiences that will provide the challenge, variety, and fulfillment they crave. It's like Alexander the Great, who reportedly sat down and cried because he believed there were no new worlds to conquer.

Obviously, work cannot be expected to cover every need level on Maslow's hierarchy. If that were possible, people would rather work than do anything else—which isn't very likely. Nevertheless, people who are well matched with their work find that their jobs can go far toward covering Maslow's two lowest needs (physiological and safety needs) and can also contribute—along with other experiences, pursuits, and relationships—to fulfilling his three higher-order needs as well. Managers at every level are challenged to create the kind of corporate culture and working environment that helps people who are basically well matched with their work satisfy as much of those higher needs as possible on the job. As mentioned earlier, teamwork can help employees satisfy some of their social needs, while a suggestion system that acknowledges and pays cash rewards for improvements in work processes and products could simultaneously help to satisfy a combination of physiological, esteem, and self-fulfillment needs.

A Motivator's Tool Kit

When the chemistry is right between people and their jobs, various motivational tools may cause them to put their best efforts behind what they do. Each of these tools is in synch with McGregor's, Herzberg's, and Maslow's theories of motivation.

Delegate Authority

Delegation, which you learned about in Chapter 7, can be a motivating force when it's applied at the right time, in the right place, to employees who basically like their jobs.

Delegating authority is one of the most powerful and meaningful ways that managers can express their faith and confidence in people. Symbolically, delegation says "I trust you," "I believe you'll do your best," and "I think you'll use sound judgment," all of which makes you a Theory Y manager according to Douglas McGregor.

Delegated authority also provides some of Frederick Herzberg's motivational factors. For example, authority gives employees an opportunity to grow within their jobs, test their own ideas, expand their skills and know-how, and gain experience that helps them become more confident, competent, and promotable. Delegation can be an exhilarating and highly motivating experience; giving people authority makes them feel important, respected, trusted, and valued, which goes far toward satisfying Abraham Maslow's esteem and self-fulfillment needs.

Give Praise for Work Well Done

A well-deserved pat on the back at the right moment can be motivating. People know when they've exceeded expectations, and they hope their boss will recognize their efforts. Sincere praise and congratulations for outstanding performance stimulate some workers to increase their attempts to exceed their personal best.

Job Enlargement

Full-scale job enlargement requires top-down management commitment and support. Depending on your operations, authority, and budget, however, you might be able to enlarge some jobs under your control in a limited way and enhance your employees' performance accordingly.

Job enlargement changes a job's content and breadth to make it more meaningful. For example, instead of having employees assemble several parts, you could enlarge their jobs by having them build entire units, run quality-assurance tests, repair any defects, and put their names on each unit before sending it on to the next department. Enlarged jobs are more satisfying; people feel gratified by the closure that comes from doing a comprehensive set of tasks from start to finish.

If you think that job enlargement requires a change in training and compensation, you're probably right. Employees who are given more responsibility must be trained to handle the additional tasks, and they'll rightfully expect to be paid for the increased responsibility. For this reason, job enlargement may not fall entirely within the scope of your authority. The concept has outstanding motivational potential, however, and many organizations have used it with excellent success.

Participative Management

This motivational tool can be used by any manager who decides to let employees have a greater voice in decisions that affect their jobs or the structure of the work itself. Participative managers lead democratically. They let their people have a say in relevant decisions, and many employees will be motivated to exercise more initiative and creativity because they know the boss will listen and respond to what they have to say.

Faced with the prospect of laying off employees to stay profitable in a recession, managers at a small glass manufacturing company took the situation to the rank and file. "We have to cut costs by X percent," they said. "The traditional way to do this is to lay off some of our people, but we don't want to do that if you can find another way. If you can recommend any workable way to cut costs as much as we need to, just tell us; we'll listen."

The employees met on their own time, discussed the problem, and finally suggested that everyone take a voluntary pay cut. Although this meant less money, at least they knew they'd all have a job and the company would be able to show a profit. Management agreed, and the business survived without laying off a single person.

Job Rotation

Job rotation trains people to perform several different jobs within their area so they can swap responsibilities and cover for each other when some are absent or on vacation. Although job rotation obviously gives managers greater flexibility when making job assignments, the technique has considerable motivation potential, too. Employees who can do several jobs instead of just one may be more enthusiastic and motivated because of the variety. It's motivating to escape the same daily grind. The occupational agility that comes from job rotation makes people interchangeable parts in the best sense of the term. Knowing they can rotate among several jobs often prompts employees to invest more effort and zeal in what they do. There's also the motivating influence that comes with enhanced job security. People who can do several different tasks are more valuable than colleagues who know how to do one job only.

One of the more impressive examples of job rotation can be found aboard cruise ships, where the same employees may be assigned to work at the check-in booth when new guests come aboard, run the tenders that take guests ashore at ports of call, sell bingo tickets, and also work as dancers or stagehands on the ship's entertainment staff.

Motivation and Morale

Any discussion of motivation should acknowledge the concept of morale. Although motivation and morale aren't identical, they're closely related, and one can certainly influence the other, for better or for worse.

Motivation is the tendency for employees to invest more of themselves in their work than they're required to, whereas morale is the mental attitude that they have toward their entire work experience. Moreover, morale can be expressed toward the entire company, the

employee's specific department, or the job he or she is presently
assigned to do. For example, employees may feel indifferent toward
their company, upbeat and positive about the department they work
in, and negative toward the projects they're working on right now.

Morale is certainly not the same as motivation, however. People can
have generally positive attitudes toward their employer, department,
and the jobs they're doing at the present time, yet not be motivated to
invest more effort in their work than they absolutely must.

When workers' motivation and morale are in balance, they feel
upbeat toward their work *and* they're willing to do more than is
absolutely necessary. When morale exceeds motivation, employees are
happy to come to work (perhaps because of the pleasant background
music, a nicely furnished office, or a state-of-the-art desktop computer) but may goof off at every opportunity. The reverse, however, is
rarely if ever true. It's unusual—perhaps impossible—for motivation
to exceed morale for very long. Management can't expect people who
feel negatively toward their work to invest much effort in it over the
long haul. In other words, highly motivated employees tend to have
high morale, but people with high morale don't necessarily have high
motivation.

It's important for managers to monitor the feelings of individual
employees and work groups and make every effort to minimize, if not
remove, barriers to high morale. These barriers might consist of:

■ *Higher management actions.* Higher management may make
decisions that are beyond an individual supervisor's control, and those
decisions can affect morale across the board. Downsizing, merging
two or more departments, transferring certain manufacturing jobs to
low-wage plants in foreign countries, or moving one group of
employees to another location despite the department manager's
objections could seriously affect employees' morale.

■ *Changing business conditions.* During economic downturns,
employees can feel demoralized when they see opportunities for
advancement and hoped-for promotions disappear into thin air. Their
emotions may parallel those of grief-stricken family members who
must cope with the death of a loved one.

■ *Personal problems.* Some employees' lives read like poorly
plotted soap operas. Employees can feel generally depressed and alien-

ated from work owing to external problems with spouses, finances, children, health, drug or alcohol abuse, and a host of other factors that managers cannot control. Fortunately, many employers offer employee assistance programs (EAPs) to help employees who may be temporarily overwhelmed by circumstances regain their perspective and restore balance to their lives.

Chapter 10

Appraising Performance

P eople usually want and need feedback about the quality of their work. Your ability to evaluate your employees' performances objectively and constructively has a major impact on their success as well as yours. But before we go too far, let's consider several suggestions that lay a firm foundation for the appraisal process.

Managers who want to evaluate employees' performance effectively:

- Have a job description for each employee who reports to them.

- Set (or collaborate with employees to set) quantified or verifiable goals for each job wherever possible.

- Maintain or have access to records that help them decide what type of training and development activities would be appropriate for each employee.

- May create a performance diary and other records to document significant incidents and examples that may be used to evaluate employees' performance thoroughly and objectively.

- Consider self-evaluation as one potential way to gather information about employees' performance.

- Notify employees about substandard or unacceptable behavior or performance promptly and frankly.

- Refuse to draw unjustified opinions about employees based on their personal appearance and/or personalities.

- Are less concerned about being liked by employees than about informing them of performance or behavior that needs to be improved.

- Evaluate people over the entire work period instead of the past three or four months.

- Are well informed about the resources their organization offers to help employees correct and improve performance difficulties.

- Actively encourage employees to obtain the in-house and external training they need to correct performance problems and develop their full potential.

Performance Appraisal—Why Do It?

There are many sound arguments in favor of appraising employees' performance. Most organizations do so to:

- Provide both employees and members of management with feedback about the success of previous training as well as the need for additional training.

- Help employees develop and implement plans for improving their present performance.

- Decide whether rewards, such as pay increases, promotions, and commendations, are appropriate or whether disciplinary action may be required.

- Identify areas for additional growth and the means by which to achieve it.

- Develop and enhance relationships between employees and their immediate supervisors.

- Help employees clearly understand how well they have met their supervisors' expectations and achieved specific goals.

Components of Appraisal Systems

Performance appraisal systems have two components: the criteria against which employees are measured (such as quality of performance, job knowledge, and job-related behavior) and a rating scale that shows the level that employees have achieved on each criterion (such as Exceptional, Exceeds Expectations, Meets Expectations, Needs to Improve, or Unsatisfactory; a ranking from 1 to 10; or a percentage achievement from 1 to 100 percent).

Types of Appraisal Systems

Appraisal systems may be categorized as subjective or objective, and many organizations may use a combination of both.

A *subjective performance appraisal system* is one that either doesn't define the performance criteria and rating scale or leaves them open to some degree of interpretation. For example:

	EXCEPTIONAL	EXCEEDS EXPECTATIONS	MEETS EXPECTATIONS	NEEDS TO IMPROVE	UNSATISFACTORY
Time management	____	____	____	____	____
Attitude	____	____	____	____	____
Job knowledge	____	____	____	____	____
Communication skills	____	____	____	____	____

Notice how subjective the above criteria are. What is meant by time management, attitude, job knowledge, and communication skills? Where would you draw the line between one of the five performance levels and another? Instead of encouraging discussion about an employee's performance, subjective appraisals tend to trigger debate between managers and employees about their respective definitions of performance levels and which specific criteria should be rated. Subjective appraisal systems, then, can cause managers to unfairly compare employees to their coworkers, meticulously record each workplace incident (no matter how minor), and allow positive and negative personality traits to unfairly influence an employee's rating.

Objective performance appraisal systems are superior to their subjective counterparts because objective systems define both performance criteria and methods of measurement. Objective performance criteria might include, for example, productivity, turnover, quality, absenteeism, and safety. Ratings are based on specific objectives that the employee was responsible for reaching.

An example of a subjective performance appraisal form appears as Figure 10-1. Note that it has a set of definitions to help clarify performance standards and reduce subjectivity somewhat.

FIGURE 10-1
Performance evaluation form.

Directions: Circle the appropriate category based on the following definitions.

PERFORMANCE DEFINITIONS

EXCEPTIONAL: Employee's performance is consistently extraordinary and well above established standards. Performance significantly contributes to meeting departmental goals.

EXCEEDS EXPECTATIONS: Employee's performance is consistently higher than expectations and standards and demonstrates outstanding initiative, judgment, productivity, and problem-solving ability.

MEETS EXPECTATIONS: Employee's performance consistently meets, and may occasionally exceed, job requirements. Such performance is routinely expected of employees who possess the education, training, and experience to occupy this position.

NEEDS TO IMPROVE: Employee's performance falls short of expectations in some critical areas and meets expectations in other areas. Employee clearly needs additional development and improvement in order to meet routine performance expectations.

UNSATISFACTORY: Employee's performance consistently falls below minimum expectations or requires constant supervision. Performance must improve significantly within an allotted time.

PERFORMANCE CRITERIA

Determination: Displays perseverance, motivation, commitment, and ambition. Achieves results even when faced with obstacles.

EX	EE	ME	NI	U

Learning ability: Able to grasp and apply new job-related skills, concepts, and procedures.

EX	EE	ME	NI	U

Relations with coworkers: Demonstrates the ability to influence others over whom he or she has no direct authority. Builds support networks among colleagues in unrelated departments and applies persuasive skills as necessary to achieve goals.

EX	EE	ME	NI	U

Ability to work under pressure: Combines determination, coping techniques, and energy to maintain or improve performance under adverse and challenging conditions.

EX EE ME NI U

Decision making: Makes sound judgments and takes appropriate action using experience, critical thinking, and logical analysis of the circumstances at hand. Accepts responsibility for the results.

EX EE ME NI U

Communications: Demonstrates the ability to listen, understand, and react openly to others. Employs appropriate written and spoken communications channels effectively to achieve desired results. Written and spoken communications are grammatically and technically correct.

EX EE ME NI U

Goal setting: Sets realistic goals that may be reached with determination and conscientious, consistent effort.

EX EE ME NI U

Employee development: Evaluates subordinates' performance and potential effectively. Delegates tasks and makes ad hoc assignments that encourage their growth and development. Provides appropriate, timely feedback on performance.

EX EE ME NI U

Motivational ability: Inspires subordinates to achieve or surpass goals through appropriate motivational techniques that are conducive to morale.

EX EE ME NI U

Management perspective and objectivity: Understands the impact that decisions have on the work team, department, and company as a whole.

EX EE ME NI U

Adaptability: Responds positively to unforeseen obstacles, challenges, and opportunities.

EX EE ME NI U

Job knowledge: Possesses the experience, personal and professional skills, and other resources necessary to carry out present responsibilities effectively.

EX EE ME NI U

Quantify Performance Goals if Possible

Quantified goals are highly objective: There's little debate about whether employees reached them. Goals may be expressed as a minimum or maximum amount or an acceptable range of performance instead of an exact figure, depending on the nature of the work and the employee's job responsibilities. For example:

> "I plan to decrease customer complaints by at least 10 percent in the hardware department this year."

> "I'm going to cut scrap and rework by 15 percent this quarter."

> "I'm going to increase the number of claims processed by a minimum of 8 percent per month."

> "I intend to have no more than 2 percent of our work estimates returned because of mathematical errors."

> "I will respond to 95 percent of all e-mail from customers within 24 hours."

> "I will check voice mail from customers no less than three times a day and reply within four hours."

> "Our team will inventory between 50 and 60 percent of the merchandise within five hours of arriving at the work site."

Expressing goals numerically instead of in vague or subjective terms helps to prevent positive or negative bias on your part and enables employees to focus their efforts and assess their own progress clearly and precisely.

If goals aren't quantified, they should at least be verifiable. For example:

> "Our department's print jobs will be free from smudges, smears, broken or fuzzy characters, and uneven margins."

> "The supervisor will coordinate the work of field inspectors so that each facility is visited at least once every three months."

> "The employee will maintain the quality-assurance reports database in accordance with Policy 123.X6 of the Department of Defense Subcontractors' Policy Manual."

> "The employee will speak clearly and distinctly enough to be understood when taking customer orders by telephone."

Should You Keep a Diary?

Some managers use a diary to record major work-related incidents and meaningful, relevant examples of employees' performance that might otherwise slip their minds from one work period to the next. Such a record ensures that you'll collect information throughout the entire work period and produce a more objective, complete, and valid evaluation than if you relied on memory alone. Without a comprehensive record, your ratings may be slanted toward employees' most recent performance. (Employees, of course, may try to cash in on that oversight by suddenly shaping up several weeks before their annual evaluation is due.) A diary also accumulates most of the information you'll need to prepare evaluations in one place so you won't have to dig through files and round up material from several sources.

If you decide to keep a diary, a few words of caution are in order:

■ Keep the record in a safe location, preferably off company premises. If the record's saved on a computer disk, lock the file with a code that snoopers can't crack by trial and error. Don't use codes that others might figure out, such as your license tag or house number.

■ Record factual data about behavior and performance. Avoid using the word "attitude"; it's too nebulous and subjective. As one manager said, "I doubt that I could observe anyone's attitude, but I can certainly observe their behavior." Don't allow your positive or negative perceptions or feelings about an employee to distort your objectivity or bias the information you're recording.

■ Make sure to record positive information. If you don't make a conscious effort to include some "attaboys," your diary may deteriorate into a hit list of criticisms and mistakes.

■ Update your information daily or weekly to ensure an ongoing and consistent record.

■ Purge older information after it becomes outdated so it won't influence your judgment about more relevant and recent performance.

Consider Self-Evaluation

Some managers ask employees to evaluate themselves as a preface to the formal review. In addition to being a constructive experience for your people, this practice broadens the base of information you can use to prepare the official evaluation.

As far as employees are concerned, evaluating themselves tends to make them think more critically about their progress and achievements. In addition, they're required to view their performance from your perspective as well as their own. Self-evaluation also gives them an opportunity to inform you of accomplishments, recognition, and problems you might not be aware of.

As far as you're concerned, this practice offers several benefits.

- Self-evaluation creates a new channel of communication with your staff.

- You come across as a participative manager who both encourages and expects employees to take an active role in the appraisal process.

- Self-evaluation helps you confirm or modify your opinions of your people's performance in light of new information provided by them.

Employees may abuse or be misled by a self-evaluation policy, however, unless you make at least two ground rules.

First, require them to supply quantified (or at least verifiable) support for their own ratings. If you don't, some employees may give themselves a much higher rating than they really deserve. Refuse to accept what they say about themselves at face value. If they can't justify their own ratings, you'll be obliged to lower their inflated opinions with evidence of your own.

Second, clarify that this opportunity is a privilege, not a right. Their self-evaluation is just one of the sources you may use to make the formal appraisal more thorough and accurate.

Nip Pending Problems in the Bud

One of the best ways to help your staff members earn justifiably high performance reviews is to tell them about unacceptable behavior or performance ASAP. This gives them the opportunity to correct problems before they end up on the record. For example, an employee who suddenly starts returning late from lunch or handing in sloppy work should be promptly informed of the problem and its potential impact on the annual review. This practice is better than letting the situation drag on for several months, dropping the bomb at evaluation time, and having the upset person ask, "Why didn't you tell me about this sooner?"

Pitfalls to Avoid

Performance appraisals are subject to several avoidable hazards. You can navigate around them successfully, however, once you know what they are. See Figure 10-2.

FIGURE 10-2
Performance evaluation pitfalls.

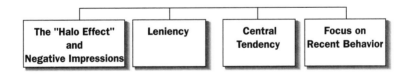

The "halo effect" and negative impressions. In performance appraisals, as in hiring, managers have to guard against forming positive or negative opinions based on someone's personality traits or personal appearance. Concentrate on evaluating how well the employee met clear-cut performance goals. That's the key issue here.

Leniency. Some managers tend to be permissive because they feel awkward or embarrassed about discussing performance deficiencies with their staff members. Although these feelings are understandable, your responsibility to level with substandard performers and counsel them about improving comes with the management territory.

Everyone suffers from a lenient appraisal sooner or later. Employees, who may know full well that they're not working up to par, can lose respect for a boss whom they consider too wimpy to confront them. The organization doesn't get a fair return on its investment in these low performers. And the employees themselves may get a false sense of security. Imagine their shock the first time they're rated by a no-nonsense manager who knows they're slacking off and tells them so.

■ *Central tendency.* This pitfall, a second-cousin of leniency, is the inclination to rate everyone's performance as acceptable. Central tendency does an injustice to outstanding performers because they're denied the recognition and praise they deserve. At the same time, their underachieving coworkers are allowed to slide by with acceptable ratings.

■ *Focus on recent behavior.* Recent behavior is easiest to recall, but it tells only part of the story. Your evaluation should assess performance for the entire period of time since the last rating, not just recent events or achievements.

The Evaluation Conference

Although some managers consider evaluation interviews a necessary evil, the information that's exchanged during this discussion can be extremely important to your employees. Most of us are anxious to know how our boss thinks we're doing, so give this meeting the respect and effort it deserves.

■ *Plan ahead.* Set a mutually convenient date and time. Tell the employee what you're going to discuss so she arrives emotionally prepared. Avoid scheduling the meeting on a birthday, wedding anniversary, Friday, or just before the employee's vacation. This gives too much time for anxiety to build. People are in a better position to address their shortcomings when they know they can attack them first thing in the morning.

Review the person's job description and records (including the above-mentioned diary and self-evaluation material, if used). Reflect on the employee's duties and responsibilities, major projects completed or pending, agreed-upon goals for the past work period, training, experience, special skills, and such qualities as job knowledge, overall work quality, planning and organizing skill, initiative, ability to work well with colleagues, problem-solving ability, and other performance-based attributes.

■ *Consider arrangements and technique.* Ensure privacy. Hold all telephone calls or retreat to a quiet location where the two of you won't be interrupted. Don't postpone or reschedule a conference unless it's absolutely necessary. Putting it off diminishes its importance and frustrates employees who naturally want to get it over with.

Some managers like to take a "criticism sandwich" approach. Open the interview by praising outstanding accomplishments and qualities, then discuss areas that need improvement and precise, tangible actions that the employee can take to correct or elevate performance in those areas. Close the meeting with a restatement of strong points. Bracketing problems or weak spots with positive feedback helps prevent employees from becoming overwhelmed by their deficiencies and blowing them out of proportion.

It's vital to criticize *constructively*. In addition to pointing out areas where employees fell short of their goals or need to improve, you must also tell them what specific things they can do to resolve or eliminate the difficulty on future evaluations. Effective performance appraisers are coaches, counselors, and collaborators. They're committed to helping people elevate their performance and reach their true potential in the future.

Avoid vague and subjective phrases like "You seem," "It appears," "I believe," and referring to the person's "attitude" (which cannot be quantified or nailed down). Support your evaluation by citing incidents, dates, times, and objective evidence of both strong and weak performance.

■ *Don't compare peers with each other.* Comparing two subordinates by name ("You should try to be more like Smedley; he has excellent initiative and is the best performer in your group") can cause trouble. Singling out one person as a role model for the rest creates resentment toward the high achiever. Instead, concentrate on how well the person you're evaluating met performance goals that were established at the beginning of the work period.

Beyond Appraisal

Performance appraisals are guidelines for success. They confirm strengths, reveal shortcomings, and highlight employees' needs for additional experience and training. No evaluation is complete, however, without guidance and direction that will help employees strengthen notable weaknesses and pursue excellence in areas that are presently sound. A complete appraisal should include a program of personal development activities, created and agreed upon by both you and your employee, that will correct weaknesses and develop or enhance future performance. These activities may include, for example, registering employees in appropriate in-house courses or seminars and encouraging them to enroll in external programs offered by the public school system, trade schools, and community colleges. The effort you invest in developing outstanding team members will pay dividends in the performance of your overall department and enhance the reputation and success of everyone involved.

Revamping Performance Evaluation: The PPG Story

In conclusion, perhaps the clearest positive evidence of the value of performance appraisal is in the story of PPG Industries, a leading manufacturer of chemicals, coatings, and glass. In the late 1990s, PPG overhauled its traditional performance evaluation system and developed what the company now calls the Performance & Learning Process (PLP). Fueled by PPG's "Challenge 2000" program to elevate performance goals, the PLP system is geared to (1) help people find ways to improve, (2) eliminate certain demotivating aspects of the old performance appraisal system and those that didn't support on-the-job learning, and (3) focus more on factors that genuinely motivate people and help them succeed.

The process was developed with input from some 8,000 executives, managers, supervisors/team leaders, and individual contributors worldwide. People at all management and professional levels were represented on the development and implementation teams. The development team also interviewed and involved in panel discussions more than 200 employees at all levels in North American and European business units and functions to ensure that the final system fully represented all points of view.

A major part of developing the new performance evaluation system was identifying so-called success factors—specific actions, behaviors, and thought processes that outstanding PPG employees believed were key to helping them achieve their goals. These success factors were pinpointed through a series of behavioral interviews with people who were identified as star performers at every level, business unit, and function. Management also looked at the success of high-performance organizations outside the company and added their success factors to the existing list where appropriate. The development team then reviewed the success factors with panels of employees and finally senior management. PLP was launched worldwide in November 1997, when management met with managers and professionals company-wide and trained them in the reasons for and mechanics of the process.

One of the most satisfying results of the new PLP process is that it enables management to connect learning with performance and demonstrate that training is not a cost. It's an investment that pays off on the job for both managers and their employees. When employees master agreed-upon skills or success factors that are known to cause high performance, higher results are ensured. Employees have since set and accomplished learning goals that resulted in their being able to sell a product or idea, solve a problem, improve a relationship, or carry out other job responsibilities to a degree that they hadn't been able to do before. The new process also calls for some minor changes in PPG's compensation system that allow managers to have more discretion to reward employees in their business units based on high performance. The system makes more money available for high performance, and places less emphasis on paying everyone at the going rate for the job.

Chapter

11

Discipline, Grievances, and Terminations

N o matter how carefully you apply the techniques you've learned so far, you'll eventually have to discipline employees, respond to their grievances, and (unfortunately) terminate some of them. Although these are among the most unpleasant duties that managers face, they come with the territory. As one chemical company executive put it, "Supervisors are rated on their willingness to assume and discharge the functions of management. [Discipline, grievances, and terminations are] functions of management." The information in this chapter will help you carry out these functions effectively and minimize their inherent stress and conflict.

Discipline

You've already learned about several practices that minimize the need for discipline: careful hiring, detailed and thorough orientation, effective leadership, and informing employees of unacceptable performance or behavior as soon as possible. Unfortunately, these measures cannot ensure that people will do what's required of them voluntarily or behave acceptably on the job.

The Hot Stove Rule

Managers who discipline employees have been aptly compared to a hot stove. They should:

- Provide warning. (A hot stove sizzles before it burns.)

- Act promptly. (A hot stove doesn't wait to respond.)

- Be consistent. (A hot stove always burns.)

- Make the penalty fit the offense. (A hot stove burns by degrees.)

- Be impartial. (A hot stove burns everyone.)

- Make no apology. (A hot stove doesn't say "I'm sorry.")

- Behave unemotionally. (A hot stove doesn't get upset or lose control.)

Stress Penalty, Not Punishment

Punishment carries a hint of vindictiveness. A penalty, on the other hand, is a cost that your organization requires errant workers to pay for the negative impact their unacceptable behavior has had on their department, their work team, or the overall organization. The damage may include lost working time, endangering or obstructing the work of colleagues, offending customers, increasing scrap and rework, decreasing productivity, or causing physical destruction of equipment or facilities.

Discipline should be corrective and forward-looking. You hope the penalty that disciplined employees must pay will cause them to display appropriate behavior in the future.

Be Fair but Firm

No matter how much you might like the wayward worker, you're obliged to be a "hot stove" manager when employees break the rules. Looking the other way or postponing your response will be interpreted as weakness or bias by the people you supervise. They may feel contemptuous toward you and hostile toward the employee whom you let off lightly.

Make policy the scapegoat for your disciplinary action. As a member of management, you're obligated to carry out all the policies that pertain to your job. Implying that you have discretion in the matter makes you a target for the disciplined employee's rage, which, recent events confirm, may become homicidal.

Don't focus attention on yourself with phrases such as "I don't understand why . . ." "I have no choice . . ." "I'm required to . . ." or "I simply can't . . ." Those "I" references make you a lightning rod for the disciplined person's hostility. Instead, use neutral expressions such as "Policy requires that . . ." "Work rules will not permit . . ." and "The company cannot allow . . ."

Precautions

Supervisors should take certain precautions before acting on an apparent breach of policy or rules.

First, if you have any doubt about what to do, check policy and procedures (especially the labor-management contract, if you're working with a union employee) for guidance on how to proceed. If those sources give you no clear direction, check previous disciplinary cases or ask a higher authority to see if a parallel situation has occurred in the past and how it was handled. If you find no precedent, proceed with care and exercise the best possible judgment. Your response to this offense may become a precedent for future managers to follow.

It's also a good idea to inform your supervisor of the action you intend to take and get his or her confirmation and support. Doing so before the fact helps to ensure that you agree and that your boss won't reverse your decision if the employee files a grievance.

Second, verify that the employee has actually violated a policy or rule. Many times supervisors who have seen what appeared to be a violation and wrongly accused employees ended up as the butt of a practical joke. One new manager who tended to shoot from the hip chewed out a group of employees at the top of his lungs when he found them working without hard hats. They smiled and chuckled, which only made him more furious. Then one of them reached up and flicked the "Hard Hat Area" sign off the wall with his finger. Someone had posted it with Scotch tape just to bait the fledgling supervisor—and he certainly rose to the occasion.

Third, take a lesson from the manager in the above example and keep your composure. Counting to ten or taking a walk to cool off may help. You can't hope to control a situation if you can't control yourself.

Fourth, make no physical contact with the employee. Even a simple conciliatory gesture like placing your hand on the person's arm or shoulder could be accidentally (or conveniently) interpreted as anything from simple assault to an inappropriate touch that constitutes sexual harassment. Either claim could land you and your company in court. If you're dealing with a highly volatile person, he or she may elect to use your well-meaning physical contact as an excuse to retaliate in kind, which could escalate the exchange into an all-out physical assault. If the situation permits, sit down behind your desk and stay there. It's harder for one party to engage in threatening physical behavior when the other party is seated.

Finally, ask yourself, "Why must I discipline this employee?" and answer that question clearly and factually. Doing so will help you place your intended action into a framework, develop a sound rationale, and avoid charges of acting arbitrarily, all of which reinforce your reputation as an even-handed, level-headed supervisor.

Disciplinary procedures will usually require you to create a record of the incident and your actions in case the employee decides to file a grievance or take legal action. One example of a disciplinary report appears in Figure 11-1.

FIGURE 11-1
Manager's disciplinary report.

To: Department Manager

From: _____   Date: _____

Re: [Employee's Name]

The following offense(s) occurred on the above date:

_____ Failure to comply with   _____ Discourtesy to customers or
grooming standards   coworkers

_____ Unreported absence   _____ Use of abusive or obscene
language

_____ Unauthorized use of company   _____ Leaving work site without
property   permission

_____ Destruction or abuse of company   _____ Other
property   _____

_____ Violation of company or   _____
departmental policies, procedures,   _____
or rules

_____ Horseplay

_____ Tardiness

_____ Insubordination

_____ Defective or improper production

_____ Reporting for work under the influence of drugs or alcohol

_____ Failure to carry out a direct order

Supervisor's Comments (Record all facts in detail)

The above offense(s) have been noted and recorded in the employee's personnel file as of the above date.

Offense Number: 1   2   3   4

Recommended action:

_____ Warning and reprimand

_____ Disciplinary layoff

_____ Discharge

_____

Supervisor's Signature

I acknowledge that I have received and read a copy of this report.

_____

Employee's Signature

Gather Evidence

Most organizations consider employees innocent until proven guilty, so you'll need to supply proof of the alleged violation. You'll look foolish if you go off half-cocked, overreact, or make vague allegations that fall apart under scrutiny.

Assemble documented evidence and/or reliable testimony about the employee's infraction from witnesses who are willing to confirm that the incident took place. This material can be critical to your case if you're called upon to defend yourself to higher management or in an arbitration hearing.

Progressive Discipline

Progressive discipline is a universal practice today. It typically starts with an oral reprimand and policy restatement for minor offenses and escalates to more severe action depending on the gravity and frequency of the infraction. Here's a representative example.

Critical Offenses

Actions that justify immediate discharge are considered critical offenses. The employee will be suspended for no longer than three workdays while management investigates the incident. If circumstances do not excuse the employee's actions, the employee will be terminated without notice. For example:

■ Theft or dishonesty

■ Assaulting, threatening, or intimidating customers or coworkers

■ Willful damage of company property

■ Unauthorized possession of weapons or explosives on company premises

■ Possessing, consuming, or being under the influence of intoxicants, narcotics, or nonprescribed barbiturates on company premises

■ An absence of three consecutive scheduled workdays without proper notification or five 1-day unexcused absences without notification in any 12-month period

■ Altering one's time card or the time card of another employee

Major Offenses

Although less serious than critical offenses, these actions require first offenders to be suspended for no more than three workdays. A second major offense will result in discharge. For example:

■ Committing two serious offenses within a six-month period

■ Safety violations that could cause harm or injury to customers or employees or major damage to equipment

■ Sexual, national origin, or ancestry harassment

■ Gambling on company premises

Serious Offenses

These offenses require the manager to place a written warning in the employee's personnel file. A second serious offense will result in suspension, and a third will result in discharge. For example:

■ Failure to use safety devices or equipment or to comply with safety precautions

- Smoking in restricted areas

- Work performance that does not meet established standards (examples: misuse of time and loitering)

- Repeated or continued minor offenses (more than three in any three-month period)

- Use of obscene, intemperate, or abusive language

- Removal of company property from the premises without written authorization

- Interfering with or purposefully distracting another employee during job performance

Minor Offenses

These are relatively insignificant breaches of policies or rules that can be corrected without serious disciplinary measures. Offenders receive an oral reprimand for the first offense, a written warning for the second, suspension for the third, and discharge for the fourth. For example:

- Unexcused tardiness

- Excessive break time

- Failure to observe a supervisor's instructions

- Attending to personal business on company time

- Disorderly, loud, or unruly conduct

- Minor damage to company property

If no further disciplinary action is required within one year of a written warning, the warning is removed from the employee's file and the disciplinary cycle starts over.

You can help your company improve its working environment and minimize turnover and grievances by tabulating the reasons for disciplinary actions over a period of time. Repeated violations sometimes indicate policies, procedures, and rules that have become unrealistic in today's business environment, are widely considered unrea-

sonable, or have been written in vague language that may be interpreted in one of several ways.

Frequent disciplinary action may also be a symptom of unclear
performance standards or information that was either poorly
explained or simply not discussed during new employee orientation
and training. In such cases, management can eliminate the need
for discipline altogether by addressing the root cause of the
problem.

The Disciplinary Conference

A disciplinary conference is second only to a termination interview in
its volatility. Since no two situations or employees are identical,
there's no seamless set of guidelines for what you should say and do.
What follows are eleven general recommendations based on common
sense, prudence, insight, and empathy.

1. Evaluate the circumstances surrounding the incident. For
example, did the offender understand that a policy or rule was violated? Does the situation tend to *encourage* infractions? (For example,
if your organization gives employees five unexcused absences each
year, you can be pretty sure they'll take advantage of them.) Might
inadequate orientation, training, or supervision have contributed to
the problem? Situations that seem to be causing repeat violations
should be called to higher management's attention.

2. Review evidence that confirms the offense and that can be
used to justify your action. This may include, for example, production
records, time sheets, samples of unacceptable work, or testimony from
witnesses. Be sure to provide dates, times, and places.

3. Follow proper protocol. Meet privately, so your remarks
won't be overheard. Maintain steady eye contact. Outline the facts of
the matter calmly and clearly.

4. Criticize the conduct, not the person. The message you send
should be, "You're not an unacceptable person, but your behavior was
unacceptable. It violated the rules of our organization, and it must
change."

5. Ask the employee to explain why he committed the offense.

Although this cannot excuse what happened, at least you've listened to the employee's side of the story.

6. Don't allow the discussion to wander off on personalities, speculation, unfounded allegations, or other "red herring" issues. Stick to the facts.

7. Define and provide examples of acceptable performance. Clarify what the employee must do to resolve the problem permanently.

8. Be constructive. Work toward correcting, strengthening, and improving future conduct, not punishing prior conduct or "getting even."

9. Inform the offender of the steps that must be taken now and those that may be required later according to your organization's disciplinary procedure. Make sure the person understands that these steps must be followed without fail.

10. Conclude the conference by assuring the employee that you're available to answer any questions about what constitutes acceptable behavior. Express your confidence in the person's ability to resolve the problem permanently and successfully.

11. Make an informal record of the conference for your own files while the experience is still fresh in your mind. Summarize your comments, the employee's responses, and other relevant information that might be important if the person files a grievance or doesn't take the necessary action.

Grievances

Grievances can arise from some situation or experience that leads employees to believe they've been treated unfairly or illegally or disciplined in a way that was contrary to established policies, procedures, or rules. Most grievances tend to arise from the following types of situations, which management should attempt to prevent whenever possible.

- Failure to promote qualified employees into higher-level job vacancies

- Inadequate or poorly maintained machinery or equipment

- Unnecessarily complicated or confusing wage and salary systems

- Incomplete or confusing communications between employees and supervisors

- Making unfair or unreasonable work assignments

- Supervisor bias

- Reprimanding employees in the presence of others

- Nonexistent, vaguely worded, or ambiguous policies, procedures, or rules

- Penalizing or holding employees responsible for productivity or quality problems that are beyond their control

- Supervisors' theft of employees' ideas and suggestions

- Unhealthy or unpleasant working conditions

- Unequal pay for the same work

- Failure to act promptly on employees' complaints

- Age, gender, or racial discrimination

- Sexual harassment

Every organization needs a grievance procedure that employees can follow to register their concerns with higher management. The fact that a procedure exists and employees know how to use it minimizes morale problems and confirms that management is committed to fair play and due process. In addition, a grievance procedure can:

- Provide a safety valve for complaints.

- Reduce employees' fear of reprisal from supervisors with whom they've had conflicts.

- Disclose problem areas in the organization that have escaped management's attention.

- Settle minor complaints before they grow out of proportion and escalate into a crisis of major proportions.

Proactive managers realize that it's best to act promptly on grievances and resolve them ASAP. In doing so, they should:

- Be easily accessible so employees can discuss concerns without getting the run-around or being buried with red tape (such as filling out lengthy forms or following a long, drawn-out procedure).

- Listen with an open mind.

- Ask open-ended questions that encourage employees to provide details and unburden themselves completely.

- Avoid expressing opinions until they've gathered all relevant facts.

- Work together to develop a definition of the complaint that's acceptable to all parties involved.

- Gather information from each party to the grievance privately.

- As with disciplinary actions, consult the labor-management contract, policy and procedures manual, and higher management for guidance if necessary.

- Consider the impact that their action might have on other departments and employees, especially if it sets a precedent.

- Meet privately with the employee(s) in question when they've reached a decision and make a forthright reply to the complaint. Describe and justify any actions they plan to take to resolve the grievance.

- Inform employees who are dissatisfied with the decision of additional steps they may take without fear of threats, reprisals, or prejudice.

Grievance procedures vary between union and nonunion companies. The grievance procedure in a nonunion company may look like that in Figure 11-2.

Most organizations have a time limit for filing appeals and reaching decisions so an issue won't be dragged out indefinitely or grow more serious because employees believe management is dragging its feet. Although most grievances are settled at lower levels in the process,

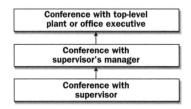

FIGURE 11-2
Grievance procedure in a nonunion organization.

steps that involve higher management should be included in case of a stalemate. The grievance should be placed in writing at the first level to establish and focus on the facts of the matter and prevent concerned parties from modifying their stories later to suit the circumstances.

The grievance procedure for unionized organizations is clearly described in the labor-management contract. Figure 11-3 shows a typical grievance procedure for unionized firms.

FIGURE 11-3
Grievance procedure in a unionized organization.

Terminations

Terminating employees is the most stressful and unpleasant task that managers face, but virtually every one has to deal with it sooner or later.

Most of the guidelines that relate to discipline apply to terminations, too: be fair but firm; follow policy and procedure precisely; and gather indisputable evidence of the conduct that makes the termination necessary. Once you've completed each step in your organization's disciplinary procedure, or if the offense calls for immediate termination, then you've reached the end of the line.

The Termination Interview

The termination interview is a classic no-win situation. The employee is going to be fired, and you've got to do it. About all you can do, then, is try to make the best of a bad situation.

■ Review your records to refresh your memory on the issues, events, and conferences that led up to and justify this climax. Confirm that policy was followed to the letter.

■ Inform your boss before you act. If the employee appeals your decision to a higher level, your supervisor may have to discuss and defend your action.

■ Some organizations encourage managers to rehearse the termination interview with a human resources department employee first. If yours has such a program, use it. Role-playing the interview helps you refine your comments, clarify your thinking, anticipate the person's reaction, and place yourself in a better frame of mind for what's ahead.

■ Notify the proper people, including your supervisor and the security department, if you believe the terminated employee may threaten you or commit bodily harm. Recent highly publicized events confirm that employees who are missing a few beads from their abacus may turn homicidal when terminated.

■ As with discipline, make the employee's conduct and your organization's policy responsible for the termination. References to yourself make you a target for hostility.

■ Deal in facts. Don't let the interview deteriorate into an argument about personality differences or a plea for leniency. ("This will destroy my career." "I tried my best but you don't like me." "I have a large family to support.") By definition, offenses that require termination have gone too far to salvage. A clean break is better than a bad tear.

■ Plan the interview so it won't fall on a Friday, after the employee returns from vacation, or the person's birthday or anniversary. The experience of being discharged is devastating enough as it is. (One terminated employee tried to rob a bank shortly afterward and was shot during the attempt.)

■ Try to limit the interview to no more than ten minutes. Hold the meeting away from your office; it's easier to conclude the discussion that way.

■ Deliver the news clearly and unemotionally.

■ The same protocol suggested for disciplinary interviews certainly applies here. Handling terminations firmly, fairly, and gracefully improves your reputation with everyone else who works for you.

■ Collect the employee's identification card, name badge, vehicle and office keys, confidential files, and company property such as a laptop computer, product samples, selling aids, and instruments or materials that the person may have used off the premises. If the person has access to computer files, cancel the password or access code ASAP.

What Happens Afterward?

Traditional doctrines, such as employment at will and firing for just cause, have been turned upside down by recent court decisions. The American Civil Liberties Union reports that the average jury verdict in wrongful termination lawsuits now exceeds $500,000. That's ample reason to handle terminations as smoothly and skillfully as possible.

Leave a paper trail to document that everything was handled correctly and "by the book." This can be vital to your organization's defense if a terminated employee takes legal action. File all the material that you accumulated on the incident in a safe place and hope you won't need it.

Refuse to discuss any aspects of the termination or the employee's performance or conduct with third parties such as other employees or prospective employers. A manager who states or even implies anything negative about a former employee to a prospective employer may be flirting with a lawsuit; the costs of defense can be enormous. Fired employees have successfully sued former employers on such grounds as defamation of character, slander, intentionally inflicting emotional distress, invasion of privacy, and even "abusive discharge."

Chapter

Communicating for Success

Communication could be defined as the act of transferring a message and its meaning to one or more people. Sounds simple, doesn't it? In the real world, however, communication can pose major challenges.

Figure 12-1 is a diagram of the communication process. In two-way communication, the parties alternate the roles of receiver and sender, exchanging messages through assorted barriers. Feedback enables each party to confirm the other's meaning and work toward understanding.

FIGURE 12-1
The communication process.

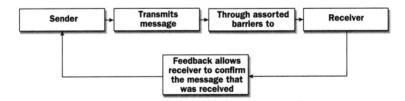

The Importance of Feedback

Communication involves three messages: the message you intended to send, the message you sent, and the message that the other party received. That fact alone makes feedback necessary so the sender can (1) verify if the message the other party received was clear and (2) eliminate any confusion caused by the communication barriers discussed later in this chapter.

You can obtain feedback in several ways.

- Ask questions to verify that the receiver understood the details of your message and its meaning.

- Ask the receiver to summarize the message that he or she received either orally or in writing.

- Be alert to nonverbal clues that indicate your receiver is confused or has misinterpreted your message's meaning.

Train yourself to listen, not just hear. Use open-ended questions and requests that draw people out and prompt them to speak their minds. For example:

"How do you feel about . . ."

"Tell me what you think we should do."

"What would you change about this if you could?"

"Please give me your opinion; I really want to know."

"I can't fix the problem until I know what it is. Will
you level with me?"

In addition, act as if you have all the time in the world. Avoid glancing at your watch or asking people to "walk and talk" as you hurry down the hall; alternatively, postpone a conversation until a time that's more convenient for you. If you want honest feedback, you've got to care enough to demonstrate your sincerity not only in what you say but also by how you look, sound, and act while you say it. If people think they're inconveniencing you or that you have more important things on your mind, they'll cut the conversation short—and you'll be the loser.

Finally, master the body language of a good listener. That includes:

- Steady eye contact

- An attentive, thoughtful, and concerned facial expression

- Occasional supportive nods and words that keep the conversation flowing ("Yes," "I see," "Oh, really?" "I understand," "Please go on; I'm listening")

Nonverbal Communication

In addition to spoken and written words, meaning is transferred through nonverbal methods. Supervisors must be able to interpret a variety of "body language," which includes:

■ *Facial expressions.* People's faces reveal such feelings as confusion, hostility, reluctance, enthusiasm, humor, suspicion, and thoughtfulness.

■ *Voice tone and inflection.* Many feelings that people reveal through their facial expressions may also be confirmed by their voice tone and inflection. For example, read the following sentence and emphasize a different word each time. Notice how inflection changes the meaning: *That's* an interesting idea. That's an *interesting* idea. That's an interesting *idea.*

■ *Eye contact.* Direct eye contact communicates confidence, honesty, and sincerity. Shifty-eyed people may be unconsciously communicating guilt, dislike, evasiveness, uncertainty, or avoidance of conflict.

■ *Gestures.* The movement and position of someone's arms, legs, and overall body attitude communicate feelings. For example, people who feel positive about your comments may lean toward you, clasp their hands on top of the desk, raise their eyebrows, or give an occasional nod. On the other hand, people who disagree with you or feel skeptical may lean back in the chair, cross their legs, fold their arms across their chests, and look through slitted eyelids—all of which are nonverbal clues that they're shutting you out.

Experienced supervisors rely in part on body language to assess employees' general morale. For example, if you see employees moving about the work area with their heads hanging, dragging their feet, avoiding eye contact, and wearing gloomy expressions, they may be unconsciously communicating negative feelings about some aspect of their work.

Barriers to Success

Successful communication can be torpedoed by several mental and verbal barriers. Once you learn to recognize them, you'll take a big step toward improving your person-to-person communication skills. See Figure 12-2.

FIGURE 12-2
Communication barriers.

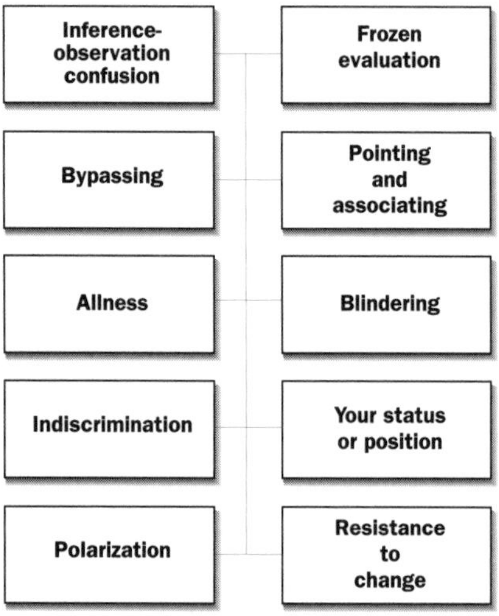

Inference-observation confusion	Frozen evaluation
Bypassing	Pointing and associating
Allness	Blindering
Indiscrimination	Your status or position
Polarization	Resistance to change

Inference-Observation Confusion

This happens when you infer more than you've actually seen (or heard) about a situation. For example, a superintendent ordered a man who was walking through a construction site to go and get a hard hat. The fellow laughed and kept on going. Then the manager flew into a rage and told him he was suspended for three days for breaking a safety rule. "Take a hike, you idiot," the guy said. "I'm just cutting through here on my way to the store!"

When Lever Brothers mailed out more than 50 million samples of its new Sun Light dishwashing detergent, some 1,000 consumers used it on salads and in drinks despite the fact that the label stated, "Caution: Harmful If Swallowed." They incorrectly inferred from the product's scent, the picture of lemons on the label, and the words "real lemon juice" that it was lemon juice instead of dishwashing soap.

Comments like "I've talked to him on the phone. He's really sharp" or "She's an excellent leader. Have you noticed how well she dresses?" reveal potentially inaccurate inferences that indicate someone's jumping to conclusions. How many employees have tried to impress their supervisors by carrying a laptop computer everywhere they go? (And have you ever wondered how many of those computer tote bags really have a computer inside?)

Advertisements that are narrated by people with cultivated French or British accents can endow products with an artificially exclusive or fashionable image. Likewise, some products are endorsed by people with a down-to-earth personality, such as Tom Bodett (Motel 6) and Dave Thomas (the folksy founder of Wendy's Hamburgers), in order to appeal to people who identify with a straightforward sales pitch.

Dealing with inference-observation confusion requires self-control. The difference between what you *know* and what you're merely *assuming* can sometimes be critical. Act on facts; refuse to jump to conclusions. Challenge your first impressions by asking questions such as:

- What do I know for a fact about this situation?

- What am I assuming or reading into this sender's message that's not necessarily true?

- What additional information should I get so I can respond rationally?

Bypassing

Bypassing happens when a sender and receiver miss each other with their meanings. It may happen if they use identical words that they define differently or if they use different words that they define the same way. In the first case, they may think they agree when they actually don't. In the second case, they may think they *disagree* when they actually don't.

People who succumb to bypassing believe that words have fixed meanings. They also tend to be poor listeners. Here are a few examples of bypassing at work:

> A police officer asked a customer who was injured in a bar brawl, "Were you cut in the fracas?" "No," she replied, "just above it."

Asked to apologize for calling his colleague an ass, one legislator purposely employed bypassing when he said, "It is alleged that I called my esteemed colleague an ass. This is true, and I'm sorry for it."

A report issued by a top manager in a government agency stated that one prisoner in a job placement program had been "reincarnated." Follow-up revealed that he had been *reincarcerated* (sent back to jail).

Motorists who fill out insurance claim forms have sometimes made odd statements that were caused by bypassing:

"In my attempt to kill a fly, I drove into a telephone pole."

"I had been driving for forty years when I fell asleep at the wheel."

"The pedestrian had no idea which way to go, so I ran over him."

"The guy was all over the road. I had to swerve a number of times before I hit him."

Bypassing also accounts for miscommunication in the following church bulletin announcements:

"This afternoon there will be a meeting in the South and North ends of the church. Children will be baptized at both ends."

"This being Easter Sunday, we will ask Mrs. Lewis to come forward and lay an egg on the altar."

"A bean supper will be held on Tuesday evening in the church hall. Music will follow."

"For those of you who have children and don't know it, we have a nursery downstairs."

Bypassing can cause expensive disasters, of course. For example, a Lockheed Martin commercial *Titan 3* rocket failed to release a $150 million Intelstat satellite from its upper stage because the craft was wired to carry two satellites instead of one. Technicians and computer software engineers who worked on the rocket fell prey to bypassing when they communicated with each other about their respective tasks. According to a company spokesperson, "No one was goofing off or being secretive. It was language that each group thought meant the same thing."

How can you avoid bypassing? Try these four techniques.

1. Restate your most important points using different words. People who didn't catch your meaning the first time may understand the second time, when you use fresh language.

2. Ask open-ended questions that *presume* your receiver didn't understand and encourage him or her to say so:

> "*What* have I said that we need to talk about more?"
>
> "*Which* points need clarification?"
>
> "I probably spoke too fast or skipped over something important, so *let's take a few minutes to talk about this more.*"
>
> "*How* can I set this up so we both understand each other?"

Such open-ended questions, asked sincerely and with an encouraging attitude, are very important. Closed-ended questions ("Do you understand?" "Are there any questions?") may be met with silence, especially when you're working with a group. People often won't admit their confusion or misunderstanding because they're afraid you or their coworkers will tease them or think they're stupid.

3. If you're communicating in writing, follow up an important memo or report with an individual or group question-and-answer session to let people talk about their concerns and possible misunderstandings.

4. If you're on the receiving end of a message, use a reflective summary. That is, restate and feed back to the sender what you heard in your own words. The sender's response to your reflective summary will help you confirm if there's a meeting of the minds.

Allness

People who fall prey to allness assume that they know everything that's important about a subject. Bad mistake! Someone once said, "For every complex problem there's a simple answer, and it's wrong." Beware of oversimplifying an issue or assuming you're an expert just because you had some experience with it. If you find yourself saying that you "know all about" the jobs your people do just because you came up through the ranks, you may be wrong. Changing technology and techniques may have made your once-expert knowledge obsolete.

Indiscrimination

Indiscrimination causes managers to be so preoccupied with similarities that they ignore important differences. They may fail to discriminate, for example, among the unique ideas or approaches that diverse employees bring to the job; the kinds of work experience or development opportunities that motivate certain workers; or specific customers' needs and expectations. Victims of indiscrimination tend to view many situations as routine, treat people as cookie-cutter clones of each other, and take a by-the-numbers approach to solving problems. A manager who says, "People are the same everywhere you go" is a potential victim of indiscrimination.

Polarization

Polarization happens when people treat a contrary situation where there is room for compromise as if it were a contradictory situation where there is no room for compromise. Either/or situations are rare. It's important to recognize that compromise and negotiation are usually possible, even if you and the other party seem hopelessly deadlocked and polarized at the start. Many out-of-court settlements, hostage negotiations, and labor agreements were concluded by compromise despite the fact that the disputes may have started with one side's offering the other an either/or choice.

Guard against polarization by reminding yourself that some middle ground is usually possible; you just have to keep digging—and communicating—until you uncover it. This effort shifts a dispute from a potential win-lose situation to at least a modified win-win situation, where neither you nor the other person ends up a loser. After rejecting someone's original take-it-or-leave-it offer, you might (1) say that the choice is unacceptable and ask him or her to propose additional ones (2) ask for time to consider the offer, then come back and propose several alternatives of your own or (3) question the other person to see if there are some other options he or she may have held back in case you rejected the one that was presented first.

The person who declares "If you're not with me, you're against me" might be wiser to say, "Let's sit down and work out a compromise on parts of the issue where we disagree." Other comments that reflect polarization (but that may in fact leave room for compromise) are "Take it or leave it," "It's now or never," "Love me or leave me," and "Your place or mine?"

Frozen Evaluation

Here you form an opinion, "freeze" it in time, and assume that the condition or situation will never change. Saying that "you can't teach an old dog new tricks" or considering someone you hired inexperienced (although you may have hired the person two years ago) means you're a frozen evaluator.

Time changes all the circumstances and people that affect your job. Dating a situation or event by asking exactly when it happened, how much time has passed, and which conditions may have changed since then can give you a very different perspective.

Pointing and Associating

Pointing labels things, and those labels may call up positive or negative associations. These associations are often stereotypes that may be inaccurate or confusing. Read the following list of words and ask what associations each one has for you.

Liberal	Egghead
Longhair	Jock
White	Hippie
Black	Nerd
Radical	Wall Street sources
Generation X	Republican
Gay	Democrat
Straight	Rapper

Techie	The government
Gearhead	Personal injury lawyer
Redneck	Environmental activist
Washington	

Words themselves can create prejudicial associations, depending on what they point your thoughts toward. This condition has encouraged the growth of doublespeak, jargon, and "politically correct" gobbledygook that dulls the edge of clarity. Thus an "antipersonnel weapon" is one that kills people; someone may be "dehired" instead of fired; companies have recently "downsized," "rightsized," or made a "skill-mix adjustment" or "chemistry change" instead of laying off employees; hospitals have reported "negative patient care outcomes" instead of deaths and "nonfacile manipulation of a newborn" when a clumsy nurse drops an infant on the delivery room floor. Insurance salespeople often call funeral and burial expenses "final costs" that must be paid after you "expire" or "transition" (die). There are no bad drivers working for one large parcel-delivery company. Management calls them the "least best."

You may have noticed that pointing and associating and inference-observation confusion seem closely related. Pointing and associating occur when people react in prejudicial ways to words, phrases, or comments that have significant associations for them. Inference-observation confusion has a broader base. It occurs when people jump to faulty and unjustified conclusions.

The following whimsical list cuts through the barrier of pointing and associating by translating vague or positive-sounding statements into more forthright terms.

We're making a survey.	We need more time to think of an answer.
We're working on the problem.	We just found out about it.
Use your own judgment.	If you want to take the risk, that's fine. Just don't involve me.

This was an administrative over- sight.	I really screwed up.
This information is in error.	I don't want to tell you who screwed up.
Let's get together on . this.	I assume you're as confused as I am.
I want to be sure we all agree.	If this doesn't work, I want to spread the blame around.

If you want to test your susceptibility to pointing and associating, just ask yourself, "Which weighs more, a pound of lead or a pound of feathers?"

Blindering

This communication barrier arises when people allow their thoughts or actions to be restricted by artificial boundaries. You can protect yourself against blindering by challenging apparent restrictions or limits. Sometimes, you'll be pleased to discover, they may not be as confining as they seem. For example, policies and rules are written on paper, not carved in stone. It's possible that some of them could be changed to let you take some action that's presently prohibited. Moreover, tradition may cause people in your organization to keep on doing things "the way we've always done it" out of habit when simpler, faster, or easier ways are available—and perfectly acceptable, if you realize that you've let yourself be restricted by something that's not really an obstacle at all.

Your Status or Position

Have you ever glossed over a problem when you had to tell your boss about it? If so, you can appreciate how someone's formal position can erect a communication barrier. The higher one's position in an organization, the more others may tend to tell that person half-truths or what they think he or she wants to hear.

Managers at every level must work hard to convince employees that they won't shoot messengers who bring bad news. Keep yourself approachable. Employees must feel free to tell you the whole story without fear of being handed their heads.

Resistance to Change

Sometimes a message is rejected or not fully understood because the receiver is too busy worrying about the change that the sender's announcing.

Changes are uncertain, strange, unsettling, uncomfortable, and a break with the old and comfortable way of doing things. The tendency to fear and resist change keeps people from fully understanding management's reasons for the change, its potential benefits, and the steps by which it will be brought about.

Speaking Versus Writing

Now that you can recognize several major communication barriers, let's look at your two choices of media. When should you send a message orally, and when should you put it in writing? Your choice will be affected in part by how much time you have, how important the message is, the attitude and nature of your intended receiver(s), and whether you want to keep a permanent record.

You may want to send a message orally instead of putting it in writing when:

- You want immediate and direct feedback. Speaking face-to-face enables you to ask questions, confirm the receiver's understanding, and provide clarification.

- You don't want a written record. If writing will commit you too firmly to a course of action and take away your options or flexibility, you may not want to create documents that could come back to haunt you.

- There's not enough time to put something in writing.

- Delivering the message in person will increase its impact or urgency.

You may want to write a message if:

- Several people must act on the same instructions.

- There are regulatory, legal, or contractual requirements involved.

- You want to take a formal position on the matter, clarify an opinion, or dispel a rumor.

- You want to provide a precise set of instructions.

- The receiver tends to disregard or forget oral instructions.

Giving Directives

There's more to directing than just telling people what you want them to do. To make your intentions known, you should:

- Be clear and definite. People should know precisely what you want them to do.

- Provide reasons when appropriate so employees can respond intelligently and place this new directive in priority with your earlier ones.

- Demonstrate or illustrate the results you expect.

- Provide enough details to eliminate ambiguity or confusion.

- Verify that the directive is within policy and the employee's job description if the person expresses concern or reluctance.

- Assign a deadline if necessary.

- Respect employees' dignity. Don't "talk down" to them, treat them like robots, or overemphasize your formal authority.

- Encourage employees to ask questions about any part of the assignment and about problems that may arise after the job gets under way.

You can choose from one of four directive formats, depending on the circumstances.

1. A *suggestion* is the least forceful type of directive. Employees may respond to a suggestion ("Why don't you try to get this order packed and shipped by Thursday morning?") if your people are perceptive and responsive enough to realize that this suggestion should be taken to heart because it comes from you, their manager.

2. A *request* is more direct than a suggestion. Here you point-edly ask someone to do the job ("Will you see to it that this order is packed and shipped by Thursday morning?"). Requests are usually forceful enough to get your point across.

3. A *command* or *direct order* may be required in emergencies, when time is short, if employees are lazy or indifferent, or when you're assigning unpleasant work ("Jack, even though this order may be awkward to pack and ship, I want you to get it out by Thursday morning. Do you understand?"). Because of their dictatorial nature, commands should be used sparingly.

4. A *call for volunteers* may be fitting if the job is unusual or unpleasant and several employees are equally qualified and eligible to do it ("We have to get this order packed and shipped by Thursday morning. I'd like one volunteer to get on it right away"). Of course, if no one volunteers, you'll have to resort to a request and maybe even a direct order.

Listening Tips

Listening is hearing with a purpose. When you sharpen your listening skills, you can do more in less time, compliment and flatter others with your attention and interest, and eliminate mistakes caused by receiving incorrect or incomplete information.

Here are five basic tips to make you a more efficient and effective listener.

1. Listen positively. Try to learn something from what the speaker says.

2. Listen with a sensitive ear. Empathize with the speaker. Don't assume that he or she understands your problem or point of view.

3. Evaluate and analyze what you hear. Challenge the speaker's comments. Are they logical? Does the speaker supply credible support for them? Do they make sense? Distinguish between "nice to know" and "need to know" information.

4. React to what you hear. Ask questions; summarize main points silently or repeat them back to the speaker; compare, contrast, and draw analogies.

5. Adjust to the speaker. Get in tune with the person's gestures, facial expressions, pauses, secondary remarks, humorous quips, and rate of speech. Don't listen at one pace to what's being said at another.

Basic Business Writing Tips

Everything you write says something about yourself as well as your subject. Expect other people to judge you by the quality of your writing because that's often all they have to go on. David J. Buerger of Santa Clara University observed, "[with the advent of electronic mail], managers send and receive messages on a one-to-one basis. Now that secretaries don't fix their sloppy writing, the whole world wonders how they passed English 1A."

How can you write better letters, memos, and reports? Try these basic steps.

Make an Outline

A polished and detailed outline is the first step toward a relatively painless piece of writing. Since you're preparing the outline for your eyes only, don't worry about being fancy. Just set down key points, supporting material, examples, and details in the most logical order you can; then let your outline incubate. Think about material that might be added, combined, expanded, or cut. Jot down ideas in a pocket notebook for future reference.

After you've pondered your outline for a while, rewrite it and insert material that you thought of during incubation. Ask questions such as:

■ Have I covered the information logically?

■ Do I have enough details and examples to support the points I want to make?

■ Have I cut irrelevant details and unnecessary information?

In addition, make certain you understand whom you're writing to and why by asking such questions as:

- Why am I writing this document?

- What point(s) do I want to make?

- How much does the reader already know?

- What can the reader expect to learn from this?

- What questions will I try to answer, or what problems will I try to solve?

- How should I organize and present the material to get the most positive reaction from the person I'm writing it for?

- What complaints or criticisms have I heard this reader make about written work she received from others? (Possible examples include: poor spelling, grammar, sentence construction or organization; too much or too little detail; insufficient data to support suggestions or recommendations; not enough visual aids; citing statistics with no references.)

These questions aren't meant to imply that you should do a snow job on the person or people you're writing to, only that you should acknowledge your receiver's likes and dislikes, prejudices, and priorities if you want to make the best possible impression.

Write a First Draft

Once your outline's hammered into shape, write a first draft. Don't worry about sounding like Ernest Hemingway. Just convert your outline into paragraphs. Polishing and editing come later.

Let your first draft incubate for a day or so while you reflect on how you might improve it. Test for clarity with such questions as:

"What do I really want to say?"

"What sounds ambiguous, vague, or confusing?"

"What questions have I left unanswered?"

Ask yourself how you'd explain the subject to your spouse, a new trainee, or someone else who knew nothing about it. Here are six additional guidelines:

1. Think about whom you're writing for. What does that person expect you to say? Would charts, graphs, diagrams, and other visual aids help you make your points more clearly and vividly? If so, put them in.

2. Avoid the urge to make your work "sound like" a memo or report. Don't let your education or job knowledge get in the way of what you're trying to say. Use simple words and plain language; your busy supervisor will thank you for it.

3. Use active voice instead of passive voice. When it comes to writing, active voice is chili; passive voice is oatmeal. Write *to* your readers, not *at* them. Which of the following sounds best?

   "Higher management wants us to change the way we requisition office supplies."

   "We have been requested by higher management to conduct a revision of the system by which office supplies are requisitioned."

4. When you have several points to make, consider putting them in a numbered or bulleted list (like this one) instead of burying them in text. Lists are easier for people to read and understand.

5. Pay attention to mechanics such as spelling, grammar, and sentence construction. Keep sentences brief—about twelve to twenty words—for maximum impact.

6. De-sex your writing. In today's business setting, writers can't get away with using "he" to refer to both men and women. Likewise, it's awkward to riddle a memo with "he/she" or "he or she" as a way to address both sexes. Instead of using the singular person, client, customer, or

employee (which forces you to use he/she or he or she later), "pluralize" your work by saying people, clients, customers, or employees. Then you can refer to them collectively as "they" and "them."

Edit

As you edit your first draft (and later drafts), be on the lookout for unsupportable claims or broad generalizations such as "It's common knowledge . . . ," "Most people believe. . . ," or "Everyone says . . ." Provide references for statistics and other data to give your work a tone of authority and accuracy. Convert dull, pompous passive voice and "businessese" phrases to active voice. For example:

Instead of	**Say**
We are in receipt of	We received
Relative to	About
It has come to my attention	I recently discovered
It is the opinion of	I (we) believe
On the occasion of	When/During/On
In view of the fact that	Since/Because
In the event that	If

Once you've edited the piece a couple of times, read it aloud. Try to hear it through the ears of your recipient. Listen for rhythm, clarity, and overall quality.

Pay strict attention to fundamentals of spelling, grammar, sentence construction, and proper word usage. Sound-alike words can turn a serious memo into a belly laugh: one manager recommended purchasing a vehicle with a heavy-duty "wench" on the front; another expressed concern about employees' "moral" problems.

If you're not sure about a word's definition, check your dictionary. Remember the example of the person who had been "reincarnated"? Computer spell-checking programs won't check for proper usage.

If you're writing an especially detailed or technical piece, read your first draft aloud or read it into a tape recorder and play it back. How does it sound? Does it fit together and flow smoothly? Are your main points presented logically? Do they support what you're trying to say?

Rewrite

Since clean copy is easier to read and edit, rewrite your first draft after a couple of editorial passes and print a second draft. Then repeat the process again. A piece of writing improves a little bit with every editing pass.

How many editing and rewriting cycles should you go through? There's no magic number. Edit and rewrite until you've said what you want to say as clearly and effectively as possible, then proofread the work word for word and line by line.

It's safe to assume that every draft of your written work has at least one error that you haven't discovered—and it could be a disaster. For example, one manager sent out hundreds of copies of a form letter that began, "In these days of educational buzzards . . ." His secretary heard the dictated phrase "buzzwords" as "buzzards," and the spelling checker gave it a clean bill of health. A stockroom supervisor reported that the office supplies inventory included an oversupply of "onions kin" paper; boating regulations posted at one Orlando, Florida, launch ramp prohibit passengers from riding on a boat's "gun whale."

Also make sure that your final draft provides closure. If your writing requires a response, don't leave the recipient in limbo. Assign responsibility, request action, set a deadline, or provide a timetable for follow-up. Ask the question, "What should happen next?" and answer it so that your reader knows what to do without contacting you.

Say It Right: Tips for Clear, Effective Speaking

It's not enough just to write clearly. Effective supervisors need to enhance their spoken communications skills, too.

Demonstrate

Showing and telling beats telling alone. Demonstrate what you're saying by giving people a model or example to help them confirm whether they've done the job correctly. Demonstrating saves you time; employees won't be as likely to interrupt you by asking you to check what they've done because you've given them a way to check it themselves.

Provide Adequate Details

Make sure that employees understand the *why* behind the *what* so they can carry out your directives intelligently. Providing adequate details can be challenging, however, because some people will grasp your meaning faster and with less explanation than others. Use the feedback techniques discussed earlier in this section to help you decide whether you've given someone enough details or if you should elaborate more on what you've said.

Consider Setting a Deadline

You may want to give employees a deadline for completing tasks that must be done as soon as possible. A deadline prompts them to focus their energy and manage their time to ensure that everything comes together as it should.

Show Respect

Respect people's dignity and intelligence when you speak to them. Avoid talking down to them or sounding like you're giving them their marching orders. Effective speakers realize that the impression they create and the results they get depend both on what they say and how they say it.

Provide Reasons

Giving a rationale or justification for an assignment confirms that it's important—and worth the employee's time. Assure the person that the task isn't just busywork. Verify how the job fits into your department's overall work, and it will move all of you closer to your goals.

Speaking to Groups

Although most spoken communication is one-on-one, it's also important to develop and enhance your public speaking skills. Here are six tips for speaking to groups:

1. Avoid repeating filler words and crutches such as "like," "you know," "ah," and "um" to avoid silence. Sometimes a simple pause can be a powerful way to capture people's attention or sharpen their curiosity.

2. Maintain steady eye contact. Make everyone in the room feel important by talking *to* them. Don't look over their heads, read from your notes, or talk to the ceiling.

3. Develop lively, colorful audiovisual materials, such as overhead projector transparencies, handouts, and posters, that reinforce and add value to your speech. Communicate through your listeners' eyes as well as their ears.

4. Profile your audience. What background, experience, and education do they have? What information will they expect to learn from you? What questions will they probably ask?

5. Keep your notes brief. Number the cards or pages clearly so you can keep them in the proper order. Identify the points where you'll insert transparencies or other visual aids. Use a large type font so you can read your notes from a distance.

6. Rehearse, rehearse, and rehearse. Read your speech into a tape recorder. Play it back to critique your voice inflection, listen for filler words and crutch phrases, and assess your rate of delivery. Practice in front of a mirror to perfect gestures and facial expressions.

Index